HOMICIDE

HOMICIDE

A SCREENPLAY BY
DAVID MAMET

GROVE WEIDENFELD

New York

Published by Grove Weidenfeld
A division of Grove Press, Inc.
841 Broadway
New York, NY 10003-4793

Published in Canada by General Publishing Company, Ltd.

Library of Congress Cataloging-in-Publication Data

Mamet, David.
Homicide : a screenplay / by David Mamet. — 1st ed.
p.   cm.
ISBN 0-8021-3308-8 (acid-free paper)
I. Title.
PN1997.H616   1992
791.43′72—dc20   91-33891
                                                        CIP

Manufactured in the United States of America

Printed on acid-free paper

Designed by Irving Perkins Associates

First Edition 1992

1   3   5   7   9   10   8   6   4   2

To the memory of my father

CAST

The Homicide Squad

BOB GOLD	*Joe Mantegna*
TIM SULLIVAN	*William H. Macy*
LIEUTENANT SENNA	*Vincent Guastaferro*
JILLY CURRAN	*J. J. Johnston*
FRANK	*Jack Wallace*
OLCOTT	*Lionel Mark Smith*
CATHY BATES	*Roberta Custer*
DOUG BROWN	*Charles Stransky*
JAMES	*Bernard Gray*
COMMISSIONER WALKER	*Paul Butler*
MR. PATTERSON	*Louis Murray*

At the Police Station

WALTER B. WELLS	*Colin Stinton*
DESK SERGEANT	*Chris Kaldor*
SERGEANT GREEN	*Linda Kimbrough*
RECORDS OFFICER	*Robin Spielberg*
REPORTER	*Yuri Alexis*
WILLIE SIMS	*Darrell Taylor*

DELIVERYMAN	*Jonathan Ridgeley*
JUVENILE OFFICER	*Willo Hausman*
OFFICER ARRAIGNING WELLS	*Leo Burns*
ROOKIE	*Ron Butler*
OFFICER ESCORTING MS. KLEIN	*Lee Cohn*
OFFICER TRANSPORTING WELLS	*George Harvey*
PLAINCLOTHES OFFICER	*Charles Chessler*

Randolph's Apartment

F.B.I. TEAM LEADER	*Jordan Lage*
S.W.A.T. TEAM	*George Rogers*
	Steve Anderson
	Elmer Aulton
	Anthony Boer
	Michael Hammond
	Guy Johnson
RANDOLPH	*Ving Rhames*
WOMAN WITH RANDOLPH	*Erica Gimpel*

At the Variety Store

OFFICER FERRO	*Tony Mamet*
OFFICER THREATENED BY DOG	*Larry Kopp*
DR. KLEIN	*J. S. Block*
MS. KLEIN	*Rebecca Pidgeon*
POLICE CAPTAIN	*Bob Moore*

CAPTAIN'S DRIVER	*Keith Johnson*
CRIME SCENE TECHNICIAN	*Alan Soule*
NEIGHBORHOOD WOMAN	*Sandy Waters*
OFFICER AT THE VARIETY STORE, NIGHT	*Cliff McMullen*
FIRST KID	*Purnell McFadden*
SECOND KID	*Wesly Nelson*
RANDOLPH'S MOTHER	*Mary Jefferson*

At the Klein's Apartment

UNDERTAKER	*Jonathan Katz*
MRS. KLEIN	*Marge Kotlisky*
POLICE OFFICER	*Jim Frangione*
CHAVA	*Natalija Nogulich*
AARON	*Ricky Jay*
BENJAMIN	*Adolph Mall*
KOLI	*Len Hodera*
BODYGUARD	*Robert Bella*
LILY, THE KLEIN'S MAID	*Gail Silver*

At the Passport Office

PASSPORT CLERK	*Scott Zigler*
OFFICERS IN ELEVATOR	*Jerrold Graff*
	Rick Washburn
B.A.T.F. AGENTS	*Jim Grace*
	Paul Hjelmervik
SHOEMAKER	*James Potter*

At the Jewish Library

LIBRARIAN	*Steven Goldstein*
ASSISTANT LIBRARIAN	*Charlotte Potok*
LIBRARY TECHNICIAN	*Andrew Potok*
WOMAN IN THE LIBRARY	*Lynn T. Weisberg*
YOUNG GIRL IN LIBRARY	*Emily Weisberg*
SCHOLAR	*Alan Polonsky*

At the Abandoned Schoolhouse (212)

YOUNG WOMAN WITH DOG	*Théo Cohan*
YOUNG MAN WITH DOG	*Neil Pepe*
BODYGUARD WITH THOMPSON GUN	*Ted Monte*
MARV	*Bernard Mamet*
LEO	*Lou Kaitz*
BARRY	*G. Roy Levin*
YOUNG BODYGUARD	*Adam Bitterman*
RADIO VOICE	*John Pritchett*
STUNT DOUBLE FOR RANDOLPH	*Chuck Jeffries*
STUNT DOUBLE FOR WALTER B. WELLS	*Sean Kelly*
STUNT DOUBLE FOR GOLD	*George Aguilar*

CREDITS

Produced by	Michael Hausman and Edward R. Pressman
Written and directed by	David Mamet
Executive Producer	Ron Rotholz
Director of Photography	Roger Deakins, B.S.C.
Edited by	Barbara Tulliver
Production Designer	Michael Merritt
Costume Designer	Nan Cibula
Music by	Alaric Jans
Associate Producers	Andy Armstrong and Matthew Carlisle
Unit Production Manager	Michael Hausman
1st Assistant Director	Matthew Carlisle
2nd Assistant Director	Karen Collins
Location Managers	Kevin J. Foxe
	Debra Donaldson
Second 2nd A.D.	Frank Ferro
Production Coordinator	Alison Sherman

Assistant Production Coordinator	Cathleen Clarke
Production Consultant	Nancy Hackerman
Stunt Coordinator	Andy Armstrong
Script Supervisors	Dona Davis
	Mary Kelly
Storyboard Artist	Jeff Balsmeyer
1st Assistant Camera	Jon Herron
2nd Assistant Camera	Steve Hurson
Still Photographers	Christopher Li
	Myles Aronowitz
Production Sound Mixer	John Pritchett, C.A.S.
First Boom Operator	Joel Shryack
Second Boom Operator	Laura A. Derrick
Gaffer	Bill O'Leary
Best Boy	Jeremy Knaster
Rigging Gaffer	Bill Moore
Electrics	Christopher L. Walters
	Stewart Stack
	William "Rusty" Gardner
Key Grip	Lee Shapira
Best Boy Grip	Rodney French
Dolly Grip	Bruce Hamme
Grips	Michael J. Purbaugh
	Matthew Craven
	Phillip Davis
	Patrick McAllister
Generator Operator/Electric	
Grip Trainee	Adam Burt
Electric Trainee	Bill Yeats
Art Director/Set Director	Susan Kaufman

Special Effects	Kenny Estes
Art Department	Kathi Ash
Unit Manager	
Leadman	Robin Koenig
Set Dressers	Howard Marc Solomon
	Liz Weber
On Set Dresser	Lisa K. Sessions
Assistant Decorator	Rebecca Weidner
Prop Masters	Lorrie Walker
	John Mills
Construction/Decorating	Stephen Walker
Foreman	
Charge Painter	Fran Gerlach
Art Department	Mark Oliver
Production Assistant	
Draftsperson	Siobhan Roome
Assistant Costume	Sheri Dunn
Designer	
Wardrobe Supervisor	Heidi Shulman
Wardrobe Assistant	Penny Mayer
Wardrobe Shopper	Terri Kernan
Hair Stylist	Terri Trupp
Make-Up Artist	Frank Rogers
Extra Make-Up/Hair	Ellen Tannen
Supervising Sound	Maurice Schell, M.P.S.E.
Editor	
Music Editor	Suzana Peric'
First Assistant Editor	Alice Stone
Second Assistant Editor	Kent Blocher
Apprentice Editor	Max Weissman
Sound Editors	Richard P. Cirincione
	James H. Nau
	Bruce Kitzmeyer

Assistant Sound Editors	Susan Sklar Friedman
	Susan Wagner
	Leo Trombetta
	Sue Demskey
Assistant Music Editor	Nic Ratner
Apprentice Sound Editor	Leslie Gimbel
ADR Editor	Rose Rosenblatt
Assistant ADR Editor	Richard Hankin
Post Production Supervisors	Cathleen Clarke
	Kevin J. Foxe
Office Production Assistant	Michelle Strong
Set Production	Charles Chessler
	Tony Mamet
	Darryl Wharton
Set Production/Medic	Lisa Abbott
Assistant to David Mamet	Scott Ferguson
Production Accountant	Gwen Everman
Assistant Accountant	Josh Ornstein
Location Projectionist	James Timothy Tarrants
Production Associate, N.Y.	Irene Devlin Weiss
Assistants to David Mamet, Boston	Catherine Shaddix
	Harriet Voyt
Film Runner	Ryan Foxe
Production Counsel	Tom Selz
Production Finance Counsel	James Janowitz
	Karen Robson
	Phyllis Kaufman
Assistant to Mr. Pressman	Michael Radiloff

Production Business Liaison, L.A.	Diana Hrabowecki
L.A. Production Assistants	Mark Pressman
	William Towne
	Christopher Otto
	Ann Greene
Transportation Coordinator	Foard Wilgis
Transportation Captain	Ronald Smith
Drivers	Steve Pollock
	Salvatore Raimond
	Francis Raymond
	John E. Simms
	R. E. Gene Thomas
	Douglas Walk, Sr.
	John Watkins
	Robert L. Willumsen
	Kenneth Ziegler, Jr.
	Joe Zappacosta
	Michael Luckeroth
	Charles E. Bauer
Caterer	Allan Stearns
Chefs	Michael E. Hernandez
	John D. Rivas
Craft Service	Susan Gotschall

HOMICIDE

Fade in: Interior—Tenement hallway—Night

An empty stairwell. A man's back comes into the frame and he begins to move along the wall. Camera begins panning with him, past the backs of several more men, all moving slowly up the wall. On the back of the jacket of two men F.B.I. *is stenciled in large letters.*

A man in a baseball cap, looking down at his watch. He looks up.

Point of view: another man, behind him the line of F.B.I. agents against the wall in the hallway. Another man is setting explosives against the door. He retreats. The first man nods.

The man in the baseball cap nods back. Looks down at his watch, looks up.

One of the agents carrying an assault rifle eases back the bolt to check that his weapon is loaded.

The man in the baseball cap looks down at his watch.

The man with the watch looks up. Holds his hand up—"Get ready."

The S.W.A.T. team don their gas masks.

An agent near the top of the stairs twists off a bare light bulb hanging from the ceiling.

Insert: One of the agents holding an electronic detonator.

The man with the watch, his hand up, points to the man with the detonator, who presses the button.

Sound of an explosion. The door behind is blown off its hinges.

Two hefty F.B.I. agents batter through the door. Camera follows into a smoke-filled room.

Interior: Tenement apartment living room—Night

A black MAN *asleep on a couch in the cheap room, a light coverlet over him. He comes awake.*

Extreme close-up: his face, as he looks toward the door.

AGENT: F.B.I., don't move!

The MAN *reaches beneath the couch.*

One of the F.B.I. assault team pushes another of the team

out of the way and fires, hitting the MAN *on the couch with a shotgun burst.*

Interior: Tenement apartment bedroom—Night

In another apartment, a young black MAN *struggling into his blue jeans and boots. A young black* GIRL *sobbing, standing in the middle of the room, holding the covers to herself.*

The door to the room is thrown open; a smoke grenade is thrown through.

The room begins to fill with smoke; an F.B.I. agent steps through the door.

The MAN *in jeans pushes the young* GIRL *aside, steps up to the advancing agent and sprays him with an assault rifle.*

The room. Beyond the fallen agent a S.W.A.T. OFFICER *points into the room.*

The MAN *in jeans disappears into the smoke as the* S.W.A.T. *team opens fire. The young* GIRL *falls.*

S.W.A.T. OFFICER: He's in the closet!

The S.W.A.T. team fires on the closet, riddling it with bullet holes.

S.W.A.T. OFFICER: Open it—open it—open it. Gimme the fuckin' light.

They open the closet door. The closet is empty.

There is a large hole in the back of the closet. The S.W.A.T.

OFFICER *peers through the hole with his flashlight and discovers a passageway.*

The passageway is empty.

Exterior: Tenement apartment roof—Night

The roof of the building. The MAN *in jeans swings up onto the roof, looks around, moves down the roof, and looks down at the street below him.*

Exterior: Street below tenement—Night

Many cars and special-purpose vehicles in the street below.

Exterior: Tenement apartment roof, continued—Night

The MAN *moves down the roof and jumps onto the next roof.*

Interior: Police station gymnasium—Day

A small, dark gym. A uniformed officer at the door. The door opens. Deputy Assistant Mayor WALKER *and his assistant,* PATTERSON, *two black men in well-cut suits, enter the door.*

PATTERSON (*to the uniformed cop*): . . . Nobody gets in.

A group of ten plainclothes detectives, perched on the gym equipment. They start to rise as WALKER *walks to the center of the room.*

WALKER: . . . be seated. The *mayor* has got every black citizen and every black citizen's group in the city tearing at him. We've got a black man who the F.B.I. is trying to lynch, and we got a lot of people yelling "Black Panthers" and "Government Assassination Squads . . ."

Lieutenant SENNA, *a plainclothes detective, speaks up.*

SENNA: . . . Excuse me, sir, if you're talking about Robert *Randolph,* he's a *drug* dealer, we've had him on our books for . . .

PATTERSON: I believe the man is *speaking* . . .

WALKER: I need this Randolph. I need to bring him *in.* Now the mayor has called the F.B.I. off the case. They're *off.* They're out of it. I need *you* to get out there, *find* this man, and bring him in *alive.* Have you got *anything* . . . ?

Two of the cops, sitting on folding chairs, seen from the back. One has his arm around the back of the other's chair. They are GOLD *and* SULLIVAN.

WALKER: Can you *give* me something . . . ? I've got "thanks," I've got "promotions," I've got *everything* for the man, can bring this Randolph in . . .

Right, frontal, on GOLD, *and* SULLIVAN.

GOLD *looks inquiringly at* SULLIVAN. SULLIVAN *gestures "Forget it."* GOLD *gestures "Why?"* SULLIVAN *leans in.*

GOLD: What do you think?

SULLIVAN: . . . They yanked you off the case *once,* they'll do it again.

GOLD *shrugs, meaning "Come* on."

SULLIVAN: It's a can of worms. Just lay back and watch it like a play.

The men in the room. WALKER *speaking.*

WALKER: I don't know what else I can say.

Beat. GOLD *stands.*

GOLD: *Sir . . .*

GOLD *and* WALKER.

WALKER: Yes . . . ?

GOLD: *Sir . . .* ? We, uh. My partner. We *had* this Randolph, my partner and I . . . his broth-in-law. A year or two ago . . . Willie *Sims.* Who were very tight, the old days. And I think that we could get to Randolph through . . .

PATTERSON: . . . you know the whereabouts of this *Sims . . .*

GOLD: Well, yessir, he's a creature of habit, we . . .

PATTERSON: How long have you known this and why haven't you come for . . . ?

GOLD: Well . . . sir . . . we were yanked off the case, the F.B.I. . . . You know, the F.B.I., you, um . . .

PATTERSON: You could have passed the tip to them.

GOLD: Well, sir, they say, never kiss an F.B.I. agent . . . 'cause, then, you might have to take him to dinner. Um . . .

PATTERSON: Hey, I don't get it, man. And I don't *get* your fucken "humor" . . .

GOLD: . . . I . . .

PATTERSON: We got a black man killed, we got, the mayor is *besieged* and *you* don't come forward, till Mist' Walker's handing out "promotions" . . . And you come out with a *joke* . . . it's no *joke*, Mister, and, it happened to a *white* man, then it wouldn't be a joke . . .

GOLD: Sir . . .

PATTERSON: Do you work for the city . . . ? Are you a member of this police force, or *aren't* you . . . ?

GOLD: *Yessir* . . . we were told to stand *down*, I . . . the Lou passed it down, this case did not exist . . .

PATTERSON: Do you have something? What do you have? We got the mayor out there hangin' in the breeze . . .

GOLD: Yessir. I'm saying, but the F.B.I.

WALKER: What have you got?

GOLD: I'm saying, I think we can bring the man in.

WALKER: Well. Then you *bring* him in . . .

WALKER *gestures that the meeting is over. Lieutenant* SENNA *and the cops rise.*

Tight on SULLIVAN *and* GOLD. SULLIVAN *shrugs "I told you so."*

PATTERSON: Who was that?

WALKER, PATTERSON, *and* SENNA.

SENNA: . . . Detective Robert Gold, he's our hostage negotiator, fine record, good cop, twenty-two citations for valor . . .

PATTERSON: Look, you got to bear *with* me, because I'm not going to eat this *"attitude"* . . . We got the city *burning* . . .

GOLD *and* SULLIVAN *file past the group at the door.*

GOLD (*to* PATTERSON): Sir, I'm sorry, if something I said . . .

PATTERSON: Hey, pally, I don't need you to wax my car, I need you to go out and do what you're paid to do . . .

WALKER: Dale, there'll be a lot of reporters out there—

PATTERSON: —listen to what the man's tellin' you—

SENNA: Mr. Patterson, Mr. Patterson, nobody's askin' you to eat an attitude.

Interior: Police station hall—Day

Camera follows them out into the hall, where WALKER *is going away, followed by* PATTERSON *and the detectives, trailing . . .*

GOLD: Excuse me, sir—excuse me—*what* did you say . . . ?

SULLIVAN *takes* GOLD *away from* PATTERSON.

PATTERSON: I said do your job.

GOLD *turns, the group turns.*

GOLD: Mister, I'm trine' a do my job . . .

PATTERSON: . . . n'you got an answer for *everything*, smart guy, s'zat it? Mr. Gold, Detective Robert Gold, hostage negotiator . . . Barracks Room Lawyer . . . Is that it?

GOLD: No, uh . . . Sir, Mr. Patterson, sir, it seems you're . . .

PATTERSON: I'm what? I'm through with you, Mr. Gold.

GOLD: Hey!

PATTERSON: Hey? How would you like to be suspended?

GOLD (*walking away, under his breath*): How would you like to be Queen for a Day . . .

PATTERSON *turns away from* GOLD, *walks back to his group.*

PATTERSON (*under his breath*): Little *kike* . . .

SULLIVAN *and* GOLD *turn back toward him.*

GOLD: What?

SENNA: Don't you move.

SULLIVAN: What did you say . . . ?

SULLIVAN, *enraged, starts after* PATTERSON, *being held back by* GOLD . . .

What did you fucken say . . . ?

GOLD *holding him back.*

PATTERSON: . . . you want to step out in the alley . . . ? I'll tell you what I said . . .

SULLIVAN: Step out in the alley? You fucken faggot, I'll kill your ass right here . . . talk to my partner that way . . .

GOLD: . . . Tim. Leave it . . . *leave* it . . .

SULLIVAN (*to* PATTERSON): . . . you know what this man has *done* . . . in the *line* . . . ?

SULLIVAN *is pulled around the corner by* GOLD *and* SENNA, *who jumps in to separate* SULLIVAN *and* PATTERSON. *Hold on* GOLD *and* SULLIVAN. *Beat.*

SENNA: Stand down!

SULLIVAN: . . . I'm sorry, Bobby . . . Fuck 'im, huh? He had any self-respect, he'd be *working* f'ra living . . . *fuck* 'im, huh?

GOLD: . . . yeah.

Beat.

Interior: Police station, homicide squad room—Day

The squad, entering from the hallway. The room is half-painted and has painter's scaffolding in it.

OFFICER: Good morning.

OLCOTT (*approaching* GOLD): You alright, man?

GOLD: Yeah . . .

OLCOTT: Fucker had no call to get on to you like that.

GOLD *is hunting in his desk for a file.*

GOLD: Fucken case, wasn't even a case, t'F.B.I. came on it.

SULLIVAN: Two-bit, two-bag pusher, till the F.B.I. comes in, turned the fucken guy into Young John *Hitler* . . .

GOLD: Hey, we coulda found him in a heartbeat—fucken F.B.I. comes on it . . .

FRANK: Gimme couple serious Irish cops, *cigars* in their mouths, go out there . . .

GOLD: . . . that's right . . .

FRANK: . . . go bring your Man In.

GOLD: . . . that's right.

FRANK: And spare me the fucken F.B.I.

CURRAN: F.B.I. don't even *put* you, Ten Most Wanted List, till they know where you are . . .

OLCOTT: Uh-huh.

FRANK: . . . n'how long you gonna *be* there . . .

OLCOTT: Who is this guy, Tim . . . ?

SULLIVAN (*reads from file*): Willie *Sims* . . . this is the broth-in-law f'our Mr. Randolph . . . We had him nineteen senny-*nine* . . . we had him.

GOLD: We had him all the fucken time . . . he's at this . . .

SULLIVAN: S'piece of cake . . . he lives at Beal's gym down on Federal.

OLCOTT: Heza boxer . . . ?

SULLIVAN: Yeah, him and *Randolph* . . .

GOLD: It's a fucken *walk*. You want this Randolph, we go down ta the gym, he's not there, we get Sims, we tail him, we nail him, we turn him over, we shake him, he gives us Randolph.

FRANK: Let's go get him.

CURRAN: Frankie, I'll meet you at the car.

  SULLIVAN *checks in his file.*

SULLIVAN: The gym don't open till ten . . . z'get the fuck outta here. Meet down the Coffee Cup in fifteen.

OLCOTT: The Coffee Cup in fifteen.

SULLIVAN (*to* GOLD): I'm gonna get the stuff.

CURRAN: Hey, don't let 'em get ya down.

COP (*in uniform*): You guys all goin' out?

GOLD: T's right.

COP: Don't forget your gun.

GOLD: For what? To protect myself?

COP: That's right.

GOLD *nods.* SULLIVAN, OLCOTT, *and* JAMES *walk out of the squad room as the phone rings.* GOLD *answers the phone.*

GOLD (*into phone*): Homicide. (*Covers phone. Pause. Into phone as the other officers leave:*) I . . . D'tective Gold. The F.B.I. has been taken off the Robert Randolph case? Our "plan"? Our "plan" is to serve and protect—can I get back to you?

He hangs up. Gets up to follow the other detectives. As he walks out, CATHY BATES *and* DOUG BROWN, *two other homicide officers, are escorting a handcuffed prisoner, the* GROUNDER, *into the squad room. He is a white male around thirty-five.* BROWN *holds a hunting rifle.*

BATES: . . . *you* guys doing in this morning . . .

GOLD: Well, dear, they put us on The Big One.

GOLD *sits on his desk, removes his revolver, takes a box of shells from his desk, and unloads and reloads his revolver.*

As he speaks, he checks his speedloaders and distributes other shells in his various pockets.

BATES: Whattaya, going out to Conquer France?

GOLD: Yeah. Whada' *you* got?

BROWN (*beginning to remove handcuffs from the* GROUNDER): Walter B. Wells, aced his wife and kiddies, this a.m., this here *deer* rifle.

GOLD: That sounds like an interesting case, and what did *you* do, *apprehend* him . . . ?

BROWN: Yeah. We got him. The Mighty Hunter.

BATES: Can we get some ink in here?

BROWN (*to the* GROUNDER): What'd you do, mistake them for a deer?

GOLD: Hey, all we got to do is *catch* 'em, we don't got to figure them out, thank God.

BROWN: You think they were a *deer?*

GROUNDER: Yes. I thought they were a deer.

BROWN *ushers the* GROUNDER *toward the holding cell.*

BROWN: What's you kill 'em for, pal? What's you shoot 'em for, pal?

GROUNDER: I did it to protect them.

BROWN: To protect them. Well, they're safe *now*, wouldn't you say?

GOLD (*sotto*): Hey, leave it, Dougie. (*He starts to arrange himself to leave.*)

BROWN: Wife and three kids. Four shots. Good shooting, wouldn't you say . . . ?

GOLD (*leaving*): See ya.

BROWN *claps the* GROUNDER *on the back.*

BROWN: Nice shooting, Old Son.

Extreme close-up: the GROUNDER. *His face screws up. He throws off Brown's hand, lunges for* GOLD, *who has turned back toward the telephone.*

Insert: the GROUNDER *grabs for Gold's revolver in his hip holster.*

The two of them struggling.

BATES *behind him,* BROWN *rushing up.*

GROUNDER: Give me the gun, give me the gun . . .

The GROUNDER *wrenches the revolver from the holster, tearing the restraining strap.*

BROWN, *trying to wrestle the* GROUNDER *off of* GOLD.

BATES, *coming up behind them, grabs a billy club off of a desk.*

The GROUNDER *strikes* GOLD *in the face a couple of times.*

He tries to bring the revolver up.

BATES *hits him on the arm with the billy club.*

The revolver drops to the floor.

BATES *steps in and hits the* GROUNDER *several times with the billy club.* BROWN *hits him in the stomach, turns him around with an armlock, and throws him into the pen.*

The doorway, officers in uniform coming in. SULLIVAN *follows.*

BROWN: That's okay, we got him. We got him.

SULLIVAN: Stupid son of a bitch . . .

BROWN, *putting the lock on the pen, goes over to* GOLD, *who is sitting down holding his head.*

BROWN: You okay, Bobby?

GOLD: He got me a good one in the head. (*He bends down.*)

Insert: GOLD *picking up his revolver and a strip of leather.*

GOLD *straightens up, looks at the strap.*

GOLD: Ah, Christ, you tore my fucking *holster*, what the *fuck* do you want to do *that* for . . . ?

BATES: You okay, Bobby . . . ?

GOLD: What the fuck do you want to do *that* for . . . ?

GROUNDER: I wanted your gun.

GOLD (*to* GROUNDER): Whyn't you just *say* so . . . ?

  SENNA *comes in.*

What d'you want the gun for?

GROUNDER: I wanted to kill myself.

SENNA: Bates, Brown, in my office—(*Nods.*) You okay, Bob?

GOLD: I'm fine, Lou.

SENNA: Somebody gettim a drink of water . . .

GOLD: . . . the fuck is *wrong* with you man. Huh? Whad' *I* ever do to you . . . ? Huh? What the fuck did *I* ever do to you . . . ? You stupid son of a bitch.

GROUNDER: I'm sorry.

  GOLD *looks over to him.*

GOLD: You tore my holster, man. N'I got *work* to do. The fuck I ever do to you?

GROUNDER: Nothing.

  GOLD *and the* GROUNDER.

GOLD: I stood *up* for you. *Didn't* I?

GROUNDER: Yes. You did.

Beat.

Thank you for your help.

GOLD: Um-hm.

GROUNDER: Perhaps. (*Pause.*) Perhaps someday I could help *you* . . .

GOLD *starts for the door.*

GOLD: Now. How could *you* help *me* . . . ?

GROUNDER: Perhaps someday I could tell you the nature of Evil.

Beat.

Close-up: GOLD.

Close-up: the GROUNDER.

Would you like to know how to solve the problem of evil?

GOLD. SULLIVAN *comes into the background.*

Beat.

GOLD: No, man, cause if I did, then I'd be out of a Job . . . Let's go to work.

GOLD *and* SULLIVAN *leave the squad room.*

Insert: GOLD's *revolver lying on his desk where it was left after the struggle with the* GROUNDER.

GOLD *returns to the homicide squad room, picks up his revolver, and heads out the door.*

Exterior: Side of police station—Day

RADIO: 69-10, 69-10 relay to 16; what is your 20?

SULLIVAN: 69-10, we're en route to the Beal's gym, Twelfth and Loomis, on the turnout to 10-11 with two homicide 16s.

RADIO: 69-10, on a 10-11.

Exterior/Interior: Car—Day

SULLIVAN *driving,* GOLD *in shotgun seat. Cups of coffee on the dashboard and a wrapped sandwich near* SULLIVAN. SULLIVAN *checks his watch.*

SULLIVAN: 69-10. Robert Randolph.

GOLD: The man's got no call to question my loyalty.

SULLIVAN: How's your head?

GOLD: . . . and he had no fucken call to get *racial* on me . . .

SULLIVAN: So he called you one, you called *him* one . . . we get to the *gym* . . .

GOLD: Sonofabitch is going to "go" . . .

SULLIVAN: Y'a, I feel it too.

GOLD: A piece of cake.

SULLIVAN: Either a piece of cake or a slice of life. You noticed that?

GOLD: Yeah. I've remarked that. Ain't that the truth?

SULLIVAN: That *is* the truth.

   Beat.

GOLD: They could of brought this sonofabitch in with a Knock on the Door.

SULLIVAN: Well, let's *us* go bring him in then.

GOLD: Thass right.

SULLIVAN: Garner some of them "kudos" and all, that they got.

GOLD: That's right.

   Beat.

F.B.I., maan . . .

SULLIVAN: . . . that's right.

GOLD: F.B.I. Could fuck up a baked potato.

SULLIVAN: F.B.I. coon't find Joe Louis in a bowl of rice. You know what's needed here?

GOLD: What's that?

SULLIVAN: "Police" work.

GOLD: Yeah. Some of that "police" work that people talk about.

Beat.

What happened to The Job?

SULLIVAN: Mmm.

GOLD: Fucken "politics," man, nothing but *politics* . . . Motherfucker called me a "kike" . . . Job's changed. It ain't the same Job.

SULLIVAN: Job's the same.

GOLD: Yeah?

SULLIVAN: People dying, people killing them. How's your head?

GOLD nods.

Sonofabitch whapped you a good one.

GOLD: Yeah.

GOLD nods, reaches over, takes a cigarette from Sullivan's pocket, lights it, shakes his head woozily.

SULLIVAN: We get to the gym . . . Hey, that sonofabitch whopped you, *mean*, you're genn' a *bump* on there.

He reaches on the seat next to him. Takes a sandwich out of a paper bag. Hands it to GOLD.

Put, the uh, put the *meat* on it from my lunch. Put the meat on it.

GOLD: You're kidding . . .

SULLIVAN: No. That's *draw* it. Really.

He turns to look at GOLD.

GOLD: Hey, what *don't* you know?

SULLIVAN: Isn't it?

GOLD: You are one smart Indian . . .

GOLD. *Reacts to something in the street ahead of them.*

GOLD: Look out—

Close-up: SULLIVAN *turns. Looks.*

Point of view: a squad car skewed in the street in front of them.

Insert: Sullivan's foot comes down heavy on the brakes.

Exterior: Street—Day

The wheels of the car, locking, skidding.

Angle: interior of the car. The two cops as the car comes to a rest.

They look through the windshield.

Point of view: a very young uniformed officer, waving at them, hurrying toward them.

Interior of the car. The PATROLMAN *comes over.*

PATROLMAN: He's in there!

GOLD: *Who's* in there?

PATROLMAN: Didn't you get my call?

GOLD: What?

PATROLMAN (*through the car window*): My partner's pinned down in there.

Exterior: Ghetto street—Day

SULLIVAN *and* GOLD *hurriedly get out of the car, taking cover, drawing the young* PATROLMAN *back.*

SULLIVAN: What is it?

GOLD: Get down! (*Reaches for his revolver.*) Where's my piece . . . ?

He feels around. Looks back in the car.

Point of view: the revolver on the car seat.

GOLD *takes the revolver, puts it back in his holster.*

SULLIVAN: Bob, what is it?

GOLD: What is it?

PATROLMAN: . . . ah, had a . . . had a shooting . . .

GOLD: How many are there, are there in there?

PATROLMAN: It's a dog.

SULLIVAN: What's a dog?

PATROLMAN: The lady was shot, we came in.

GOLD: Okay, okay—how many guys are in there?

SULLIVAN *in the background is talking on the radio.*

PATROLMAN: Guys? What guys? Just my partner and the dog.

GOLD: There's just a dog in there?

PATROLMAN: Yeah, the dog, dog—the fucken dog's tryin' to kill him.

GOLD: Shoot the dog, man!

PATROLMAN: It's my first *day*, I got a body in there. I . . .

SULLIVAN (*to* GOLD): Bob.

PATROLMAN: Give me a hand, man, just, just, just . . .

GOLD: You call your sergeant?

PATROLMAN: Just until he . . .

SULLIVAN: Bob.

GOLD: Yeah, okay. Gimme the sandwich.

SULLIVAN: We gotta roll.

GOLD: Gimme the sandwich.

SULLIVAN: Bob.

GOLD: Gimme the fucken sandwich.

He walks over to the car, takes the sandwich.

(*To the* PATROLMAN:) Okay, you calm down.

He and the PATROLMAN *walk away from the car.*

GOLD (*over his shoulder*): Right back at you. Who's dead?

PATROLMAN: Some lady. The owner.

GOLD: For sure?

PATROLMAN: Hit her with a shotgun, thank you, detective.
I . . .

GOLD: Shut up. Anyone else? Anyone living?

PATROLMAN: No.

GOLD: You call the ambulance?

PATROLMAN: They're coming.

GOLD: How long have you been here?

PATROLMAN: Two minutes.

Camera dollies with them over to the front of Klein's Variety Store, a half-store on a very run-down block of the ghetto.

GOLD: Okay . . . (*Checking the patrolman's name tag.*) Officer Ferro, get out your fucken notebook. You write down the exact time of your arrival, you, your partner's star number, I was never here.

PATROLMAN: I understand. I, thank you, you were never here.

GOLD *walks to the front of the variety store.*

GOLD (*calls*): What is it in there?

SECOND OFFICER (*from inside the variety store*): I can't move, man. Who is that?

GOLD: It's the *cops*. Okay. You can't move, *don't* move. Can you get to your piece?

SECOND OFFICER (*voice-over*): If I move, man, the fucken dog is going to kill me.

GOLD: Does he have a *collar* on, can you see a collar?

SECOND OFFICER (*voice-over*): Yeah.

GOLD: Is it a *choke* collar . . .

SULLIVAN (*checking his watch*): Bobby, I gotta roll . . .

GOLD: Fuck *me* . . . get *on* . . . Go on, get outta here. Take the car. (*To the* PATROLMAN:) Hey, go get your jacket . . .

SULLIVAN *nods. Goes to the car. The car pulls out.* GOLD *addresses the officer in the store.*

GOLD: A *choke* collar . . . ?

SECOND OFFICER (*voice-over*): Yeah. I can see it. It's a choke collar. Yeah.

GOLD *takes the patrolman's jacket, wraps it around his forearm.*

Interior: Variety store—Day

The variety store. Dark, dusty. The SECOND OFFICER *pinned against the wall. Sound of the door opening.*

A very large rottweiler turns his head to the sound of the door. The officer's legs are visible in the background.

GOLD *coming in the door, slowly, advances on the dog, holding out the sandwich, talking softly.*

SECOND OFFICER: I'm scared, man.

GOLD: I know you are. Just hang tight. It'll all be over in a minute. Nothing to it. Piece of cake, really.

The dog, growling low.

Nice and easy. Everybody's your friend.

SECOND OFFICER: Be careful, man . . .

GOLD: Atta boy . . .

GOLD *holds out his wrapped arm, advancing on the dog. Slowly he inches up on the dog and grabs the dog's choke collar as the dog takes the sandwich. He straightens up, pulling the chain tight.*

(*To* SECOND OFFICER:) Chain him, outside . . .

SECOND OFFICER: What a thing, huh? Thank you, man— thank you.

GOLD: S'all right.

SECOND OFFICER (*moving toward the phone*): I got to call. I . . . I got to call . . .

GOLD: Don't touch the phone. You got to call, call *outside.*

SECOND OFFICER: Thank you, man.

GOLD *gives the* SECOND OFFICER *control of the dog.*

GOLD: Whattaya got here?

SECOND OFFICER: Behind the counter.

GOLD *turns his head.*

Point of view: an old woman, face down on the floor, one arm outstretched. Blood on her back.

The SECOND OFFICER *taking the dog out.* GOLD *kneeling down.*

His hand, fingering a flash of gold at her neck. A Jewish star on a chain.

GOLD. *Stands up, a bit tentatively. Fingers the bruise on his head. Beat. He looks down at the woman again.*

A bloody red hand print on the counter wall. Camera tilts down to her hand pointing at a cigar box on a lower shelf.

Insert: the cigar box. He opens it. Inside is a very shiny blue Colt .45 pistol with stag grips.

Close-up: GOLD. *Beat. He straightens up.*

Exterior: Ghetto street—Day

PATROLMAN: Okay, move it back, fellas—move it back . . .

Exterior of the variety store. A crowd gathering. GOLD *comes out of the variety store. A small black* BOY *comes up to him.*

BOY: I know why they waste her, man, because she had a *fortune* in her basement, that *Jew* broad. You wan' me to help you I can *help* you, cos' I know *why* they *did* it.

The PATROLMAN *starts to shoo the* BOY *away.*

GOLD (*to* PATROLMAN): Take *everybody's* name, address, don't shoo *anyone* off, fellow hanging 'round could be the *guy*, you understand, the *killer* . . .

PATROLMAN: Yessir.

GOLD: Nobody goes in or out of the building. Don't touch *nothing* in there, you hang tight until your sergeant arrives.

They move through the crowd.

OLDER BLACK WOMAN: See, I know she had a *fortune* in that *basement*, they said, e'en when *I* was young . . . uh-huh, they finly *kilt* her.

SECOND OFFICER: Hang tight till my sergeant gets here?

GOLD: That's right.

PATROLMAN: Thank you, Detective, uh, thanks a lot, I . . .

GOLD: Forget it. (*Checks watch.*) I gotta get *out* of here.

GOLD *looks up.*

Point of view: a large Mercedes arrives at the barrier. A middle-aged well-dressed man, DR. KLEIN, *and a soigné young woman,* MISS KLEIN, *get out of the car and walk hurriedly toward the variety store.*

MISS KLEIN (*to* POLICEMAN): Let me through.

POLICEMAN: Sorry, ma'am. No one is supposed to get through . . .

MISS KLEIN *turns to* GOLD.

MISS KLEIN: Please . . . who's in charge here?

GOLD: . . . not my case.

MISS KLEIN: . . . that's my grandmother in there . . . can
you . . .

GOLD: . . . not my case . . .

She holds his arm.

MISS KLEIN: Please, let us through . . .

POLICEMAN: Folks, nobody gets by.

GOLD *motions him off.*

GOLD: Central, Detective Gold. I need a car. Twelfth and
Prescott.

MISS KLEIN: Can you—please—can you help me?

GOLD: The sergeant will be here in a minute.

MISS KLEIN: My grandmother . . . is she . . . what's happened
to her?

GOLD: Your grandmother. Owns the variety store . . . ?

DR. KLEIN *comes up to them.*

MISS KLEIN: Is she dead?

GOLD: The woman inside is dead, yes ma'am.

DR. KLEIN: Oh, God . . .

MISS KLEIN *embraces and comforts* DR. KLEIN.

Beat.

GOLD: Relay this pickup to Sullivan—soon as the car's here I'm on my way . . .

DR. KLEIN: Officer, I want to see her.

GOLD: I'm sorry, sir . . . this is not my case, I . . .

> *A* squad car arrives. *A* CAPTAIN *in uniform with a lot of gold braid gets out of the passenger side. He comes over to* GOLD.

GOLD (*under his breath*): No . . . I can't get stuck here . . .

CAPTAIN: Whaddawe got . . . ?

GOLD: Yes, sir. We got a *homicide*, elderly woman shot . . . This is the family.

> MISS KLEIN *nods that he is correct.*

CAPTAIN: The family? Who're you?

GOLD: D'tective Gold, Homicide.

CAPTAIN: *You* got here quick.

GOLD: No, sir, I . . .

CAPTAIN: First officer . . . ?

> GOLD *beckons to the* PATROLMAN, *who comes over. The* CAPTAIN *moves closer to* GOLD.

CAPTAIN: What's this family doin' in this neighborhood? I don't get it.

GOLD *looks at his watch.*

CAPTAIN: Officer Gold—

GOLD *and the* CAPTAIN.

GOLD: Cap, I got to get out of here . . .

CAPTAIN: Take this family in, hav'm I.D. the body.

GOLD: Cap, I got to get out of here . . .

CAPTAIN: Lemme run the precinct, okay . . . ?

GOLD: I'v . . .

CAPTAIN: You caught the case . . .

GOLD: Sir. My partner and I, we got something heavy coming down right *now.*

CAPTAIN: Over the boxing gym . . .

GOLD: Yessir, we . . .

CAPTAIN: I just heard it on the radio. It *happened* . . . (*To* GOLD:) You got the case. You caught the case. Do your job.

The CAPTAIN *moves off, leaving* GOLD *alone.* GOLD *walks away from the* CAPTAIN. *Sighs.*

A crime scene car arrives and technicians get out of it and start walking toward the variety store.

GOLD (*sighs, to* OFFICER): Officer—go to the store next door, they got an *office*, tell 'em we're taking it for a command post, everybody's *names*, and everybody comes downtown. (*Sighs.*)

TECHNICIAN: Whadda we got?

GOLD: We got a homicide. And there's a real pretty .45 Colt in there. I don't want it to disappear into some cop's locker. So tag it first, okay?

He stops, looks at DR. KLEIN.

GOLD (*to* DR. KLEIN): Alright. *Sir,* would you like to come in for a moment. While we're in the store, please touch nothing.

DR. KLEIN (*to* MISS KLEIN): It never stops. It never stops. Does it?

MISS KLEIN *shakes her head sadly.*

GOLD (*to* MISS KLEIN): It never stops. What is it that never stops?

MISS KLEIN: Against the Jews.

The three start in to the variety store.

Interior: Homicide squad room—Day

Insert: A newspaper on Gold's desk. The headline reads:
CITYWIDE MANHUNT FOR SLAYER OF FED

AGENTS. 'WE'LL POLICE OUR OWN BACK YARD,' MAYOR VOWS. *Pull back to reveal* GOLD *interrogating the young boys who were present at the variety store.*

GOLD: Yeah, that's right . . .

BOY: . . . because, you know, she had that *shit* down in her basement . . .

Insert: GOLD *writes on his pad:* "She had a fortune in her basement."

GOLD: The uh . . . the . . . the old woman.

GOLD *and the* BOY.

JUVENILE OFFICER: Tell him about the old woman.

BOY: Well, thass what we talking about.

GOLD: You were gonna tell me, you said you could help us find her killer.

BOY: I was going to tell you what they *shot* her for.

GOLD: Uh-huh . . . (*He doodles on his pad.*)

BOY: The fortune in her basement.

JUVENILE OFFICER: They killed her for her fortune.

BOY: That's right.

GOLD: Did you see this guy?

BOY: No, I was in school.

SECOND BOY: It was a school day.

GOLD (*rising*): Okay.

> SULLIVAN *walks by with the remainder of the homicide team, and* SIMS *in irons in tow.*

OLCOTT: Willie Sims.

> SIMS *turns to* GOLD.

SIMS: Yeah, man, I remember you . . .

JAMES: . . . we got 'em.

SIMS: . . . I remember you. You the *talkin'* man . . .

GOLD: . . . Willie Sims. How are you?

SIMS: As you see, man . . . what are they *doin'* to me . . . ? What do you *want* with me . . . ?

SULLIVAN: You missed it.

GOLD (*looks on enviously*): Mmm.

SULLIVAN: You missed it. Got him at th' gym. Just like you said . . . happened to you . . . ?

GOLD: I got pulled off the case.

SULLIVAN: *Bullshit* you did . . .

GOLD: I'm stuck, I'm s'posed to babysit this Candy Store.

They move into the hall.

SULLIVAN: It's Your Case . . . !

GOLD (*sighs*): I don't know. Yeah.

SULLIVAN: Baby, we need *you*, turn this guy over, we need the *Mouthpiece* to *sweet*-talk his ass. Lou—

MISS KLEIN: My father needs to talk to you.

SENNA: We'll take care of it— Officer—

MISS KLEIN: My father needs you.

SENNA: Will you see Miss Klein home?

OFFICER: Yes, sir.

SENNA: I assure you we'll take care of it.

OFFICER (*to* MISS KLEIN): Ma'am.

   MISS KLEIN *leaves with the* OFFICER.

SENNA (*to* SERGEANT GREEN): I need to talk to you.

SERGEANT GREEN (*off camera*): Yes, sir.

   SULLIVAN *starts to take* GOLD *into the interrogation room. Lieutenant* SENNA *walks up to them.*

SENNA: *Bobby* . . .

SULLIVAN: Lou, we're, we're about to crack this Sims.

SENNA: I'm sorry, Bobby, I got a call, downtown, you live with this candy store.

SULLIVAN: Bullshit aside, Lou, we *need* him. We're goin' in, Mutt and Jeff, and we need Bobby. We need "The Orator."

SENNA: I got the call, he's off the case.

SULLIVAN: What you call this. Loyalty?

SERGEANT GREEN *comes up to* SENNA *with a clipboard.*

SERGEANT GREEN: Yes, sir.

SENNA (*to* SERGEANT GREEN): Come with me. (*Back to* GOLD:) I'm sorry, Bobby. I got a call. The Jewish guys downtown, the doctor's got this clout. He wants you, you were there, you're his "people," you're on the case.

GOLD: I'm his people . . . ? I thought I was *your* people, Lou . . . I come up with the idea, trap the guy in . . . *Lou* . . . I come up with the *Brother* . . . Hey.

SENNA: I'm sorry, Bobby.

GOLD: Lou. I'm in it for the *git* . . .

SENNA: I'm sorry. (*To* SERGEANT GREEN:) About the procedurals, go ahead and clear them off your desk.

GOLD: You're *sorry*, Lou, what am I, a fucken Jumping Bean?

SENNA: I'm sorry.

GOLD: What? I'm your "backup" girl? (*Pause.*) I'm trine' a follow *orders*, Lou, n'I'm getting *whiplash*. (*Pause.*) Why'nt you just go send me to the *airport*. What did I do to you?

SENNA: It's nothing personal, Bobby.

GOLD: What I'm saying, Lou. P'haps it *should* be?

SENNA *shrugs. He moves off.*

OLCOTT: Kid just gave up his brother—must not like police stations.

SULLIVAN: Just gave us Randolph.

GOLD: You got an address?

SULLIVAN: Got the whole thing. Let's go get 'im.

OLCOTT: Yo, you want a vest?

SULLIVAN: Yeah.

SENNA: Where're you goin'? You're on the candy store case!

SULLIVAN: He's on top of it.

SENNA: The fuck he's on top of it!

GOLD: I'm goin' for coffee!

SENNA: Coffee, bullshit! No! You wanna run on this other

case—it's my ass. You understand? This guy is heavy downtown—don't lie to me. The candy store—you got it.

SULLIVAN: Lou—

SENNA: Nothin' you say or do can convince me, so shut the fuck up.

SULLIVAN: It's not right.

SENNA: Get outta here.

GOLD: Goodbye, Sully.

SENNA: That's right. Whattaya got on the candy store case?

GOLD: Yeah, I'm on top of it.

SENNA: Tell me.

GOLD: Some kid said she kept a fortune in her basement.

SENNA: Yeah . . .

GOLD: I got the witnesses lined up.

SERGEANT GREEN: Lieutenant, if I go back to the 212 . . .

SENNA: Yes, one moment. I'm sorry to pull you off the Flash Case, Bobby—I appreciate what you're doing for me.

GOLD: That's alright, Lou.

SENNA: I got three calls. The guy—Dr. Klein—you'll call him?

GOLD: I'm on it right now.

SENNA: Thank you, Bob.

GOLD: It's alright, Lou.

SENNA: No, thank you—I'll make it up to you someday.

GOLD: It's all part of the job.

SENNA: That's right.

SENNA *turns back to* SERGEANT GREEN *as* GOLD *walks away.*

SENNA (*to* SERGEANT GREEN): Yes? What?

SERGEANT GREEN: I'm sorry to keep going over this . . .

SENNA: That's okay, we'll go over it from the Jump . . .

Interior: Staircase, police station—Day

The backstairs—a door opens, GOLD *comes out, camera pans with him around the landing to where* SULLIVAN *is lounging, smoking a cigarette, holding the briefcase and cruiser shotgun, which he passes to* GOLD.

SULLIVAN: Fuckemm . . .

GOLD: Let's get outta here.

Exterior: Alley—Day

The homicide team. OLCOTT *is on the lookout.* FRANK *passes a sledgehammer to* GOLD, *a shotgun to* SULLIVAN.

Exterior: City street—Day

The team striding up to a tenement, holding a sledgehammer, a shotgun, an ax, variously. Camera follows SULLIVAN, GOLD, *and* OLCOTT *to a corner.* SULLIVAN *and* GOLD *stop.* OLCOTT *moves around the corner.*

Gold starts loading his shotgun. Looks around the corner at OLCOTT.

SULLIVAN: Lovely day for it.

GOLD: Alright.

Exterior: Tenement—Day

From around the corner, OLCOTT *approaching a young black* MAN *loitering by the entrance to a garage.*

OLCOTT: Excuse me, I'm trying to find this address. Do you know where it might be?

YOUNG MAN: This one right here?

As the YOUNG MAN *turns,* OLCOTT *spins him around, draws his revolver, and thrusts the* YOUNG MAN *before him.*

GOLD *and* SULLIVAN. SULLIVAN *nods "Let's go."*

GOLD *and* SULLIVAN, *sprinting across the street.*

OLCOTT *has manacled the* YOUNG MAN *to a stanchion.* OLCOTT *points up a flight of stairs.*

Interior: Abandoned tenement—Day

The three men running up a set of iron stairs, inside the tenement. They stop at an iron door on the landing. One of them tries the door. It is unlocked.

Exterior: Roof—Day

The two men bursting through the door and running toward the wall of the adjoining building.

GOLD *takes his revolver out of his holster and puts it in his sports coat pocket.* SULLIVAN *takes a deep breath, he thumbs the safety of his shotgun off.* GOLD *stops him and motions that he,* GOLD, *will go through the door first.*

SULLIVAN *nods.*

SULLIVAN: How come you always gotta be the first one through the door? So brazen . . .

Pause. GOLD *starts to go through the door.*

Interior: Hallway of abandoned tenement—Day

A narrow hallway. One door off the hallway to the left. Camera follows GOLD *down the hall to an empty room. He turns back and retreats to the door off of the hall. Beat. He kicks the door in and goes in the door.*

Interior: Empty room—Day

Extreme close-up of GOLD *coming into the frame. Stops. Looking at something.*

Point of view: RANDOLPH'S MOTHER *sitting on the far side of the room. A mattress and blankets on the floor.*

GOLD. *Looking around the room. From the rear.* GOLD *moving up on* RANDOLPH'S MOTHER.

Beat.

RANDOLPH'S MOTHER: You want to kill my baby.

Beat.

GOLD *advances on her.*

You come here to kill my child.

Beat.

Sound of footsteps.

Close-up: GOLD *glances over his shoulder.*

CURRAN (*voice-over*): Comin' in . . . comin' in . . . Bobby!

GOLD: Yo. *Come* in . . .

CURRAN *enters. Behind him* JAMES, SULLIVAN, *and* FRANK *come into the room.*

CURRAN: This the broad? Joint's deserted. The guy ain't here.

SULLIVAN: Sullivan, coming in. Where is he?

RANDOLPH'S MOTHER: . . . I should kill my *baby* that I brought into the world? White folks? Why would that be?

CURRAN: Your baby's a murderer.

RANDOLPH'S MOTHER: He never hurt nobody.

SULLIVAN: Now that's just not the facts . . .

RANDOLPH'S MOTHER: He never hurt *no* one, now you got him out there, runnin' for his life.

FRANK: We got to get to him. We got a few days to *do* it. We can bring him in. We don't find him, we gotta call back in the F.B.I. The F.B.I.'s gonna kill his ass.

OLCOTT: That's right. And they gonna cut you a deal that the federal boys want. So what you wanna do?

RANDOLPH'S MOTHER: Get out of my motherfuckin' room. Get out of my fuckin' room!

SULLIVAN *steps forward.*

CURRAN: Hey, bitch, you don't tell us. You don't tell us a goddamn thing! We tell you!

OLCOTT: Your boy killed two cops. You think we just gonna sit here and chat with you?

SULLIVAN: Fuck this, we're wastin' our time, we're wastin' our—get her up, get her the fuck up, get her out of here!

GOLD: Hey, gimme a minute, willya?

JAMES: Hey, let's drag her ass downtown—

GOLD: Come on, gimme a minute.

SULLIVAN: We got two dead cops, what the fuck are you—

GOLD: Gimme a fucken minute!

OLCOTT: A minute is somethin' that we don't got.

CURRAN: Talkin' to a stone wall . . .

FRANK: You're wastin' your time, Bob.

GOLD: I'll be the judge of that.

SULLIVAN: Why ya do this shit?

GOLD: Shut up!

GOLD (*to* RANDOLPH'S MOTHER): We got to find him. Don't do this the hard way. Look at me, now, don't do this the hard way . . . We can *help* you. It's a bad beat and you're *stuck* in it, n'it's gonna be some crying time but *our* way is the *easy* way. Listen

to me. We *need* your son. But we don't need him dead. You
want him alive, *work* with us. We got to bring him in . . .

Beat.

RANDOLPH'S MOTHER *looks at him.*

RANDOLPH'S MOTHER: You want to kill him.

GOLD: We need to *take* him, but we need him *alive.* That's the
job we were given to do. That's why they gave it to the cops,
'stead of the F.B.I. Our job's to bring him down alive. Listen to
me. I know that it stinks. I know that there's so much death in
the world. I know that it's full of hatred, Momma. I know it all
turns out wrong. Here we are; here we are, we're the garbage
men. You think I don't know that? I know that. Looking for
something to love. You *got* something to love. You got your
boys. That's something. Look in my eyes.

Beat.

I want to save your son. Before God. I want to save your boy.

Beat.

Will you help me?

Sound of a door opening. GOLD *half turns his head.*

Point of view: OLCOTT *entering, comes up to* JAMES, *whispers.* OLCOTT *comes up to* GOLD.

Close-up: the two, their heads together, as OLCOTT *leans in.*

GOLD (*sotto*): . . . not now.

OLCOTT (*sotto*): It's the lieutenant.

GOLD (*sotto*): Not *now* . . .

OLCOTT: He needs you on the phone. He says *now.*

GOLD *sighs. Gets up. He is replaced by* FRANK, *who sits down in front of* RANDOLPH'S MOTHER.

CURRAN: Time's runnin' out . . .

FRANK: That's right, Momma—

GOLD *walks to the door with* OLCOTT.

Interior: Hallway of abandoned industrial office—Day

GOLD *and* OLCOTT *out in the hall. Two uniformed officers in the hall.*

GOLD: What the fuck does he want?

OLCOTT: It's the Yids.

GOLD (*starting back into the room*): Blow them off.

OLCOTT: The doctor. Somebody took a shot at the . . .

GOLD: Somebody took a shot at . . . ?

OLCOTT: That's what they said.

GOLD (*stops*): *Bullshit* . . . Bullshit . . .

GOLD *starts back toward the room, looks in through the door.*

Interior: Empty room—Day

Point of view: RANDOLPH'S MOTHER, FRANK *talking to her.* RANDOLPH'S MOTHER *looks at* GOLD *for a moment.*

Interior: Elevator/entry vestibule/living room of Klein apartment—Night

From inside the elevator the doors open and GOLD *enters frame, passing through the entry vestibule into the open doors of the living room, where an* OFFICER *is waiting, a* MAID *closing drapes, and* MISS KLEIN *is sitting with a notebook, conferring with an undertaker. The Kleins are sitting shiva, the traditional Jewish mourning period following a death in the family.*

GOLD *approaches the* OFFICER.

GOLD: What is it?

OFFICER: They say a shot fired, some guy on the roof.

The OFFICER *leads* GOLD *into the main hall.*

Interior: Main hall—Night

Camera leads the OFFICER *and* GOLD *down the hall.*

GOLD: A shot fired. Yes or no?

OFFICER: I don't know. Din' *hit* nothing if it did.

GOLD: Who heard it?

OFFICER: The lady.

Camera pans with them into the dining room.

GOLD: The lady, what lady . . . ? Get the lady in here so she can show me.

Interior: Dining room—Night

DR. KLEIN *intercepts* GOLD *and the* OFFICER.

DR. KLEIN: I'll show you.

GOLD: Show me what, sir? Who made the call?

DR. KLEIN: I made the call.

GOLD: What are we looking at? What's going on here?

DR. KLEIN *gestures toward the kitchen door.*

DR. KLEIN: It happened in here.

GOLD *turns to the* OFFICER.

GOLD: What happened? Gemme this number right now, my partner. *Gettim* . . .

The OFFICER *goes back toward the door to the main hall, and* GOLD *enters the kitchen with* DR. KLEIN.

Interior: Kitchen/grandmother's room—Night

>   *The* MAID *covers the mirror with a black cloth.* DR. KLEIN
>   *leads* GOLD *through the kitchen to the threshold of the
>   grandmother's room.*

DR. KLEIN: There was a man on the roof.

>   GOLD *enters the room and looks out the window.*

GOLD: Uh-huh . . .

DR. KLEIN: And my wife heard a shot—

>   GOLD *moves out of the room past* DR. KLEIN, *moving back
>   through the kitchen toward the dining room.*

GOLD: Uh-huh, and she heard a *shot.*

DR. KLEIN: Yes, she did . . .

Interior: Dining room—Night

>   GOLD *comes back into the dining room, peering out the
>   windows at the rooftop opposite.* DR. KLEIN *follows behind
>   him.*

GOLD: Would she know what a shot sounds like? How would
she know that?

DR. KLEIN: My wife heard a shot . . .

>   MRS. KLEIN *appears.*

MRS. KLEIN: There was a shot on the roof, there was a *man* on the roof, back on the, a *man* on the roof . . .

GOLD: Yes, ma'am.

MRS. KLEIN: No, no . . . I'm not making it up. It happened. There was shooting.

GOLD: Ma'am, I don't know any reason why anyone . . .

MRS. KLEIN: That's right. You *don't, do* you? But I see that you feel, that, what, you're dealing with hysterical Jews . . . ? I'm making it up, is that right? We're always making it up. Is that right?

DR. KLEIN: It's alright, dear. Let me tell you one thing—there *was* a man on the roof.

    DR. KLEIN *points.* GOLD *turns his head.*

Exterior: Outside Klein apartment—Night

    Point of view: twilight. Dark, low-lying roofs. A few pigeons flying.

Interior: Dining room, continued—Night

    GOLD *and* DR. KLEIN.

GOLD: Look. Doctor—

    Beat.

Why would anybody be shooting at you?

Beat.

You follow me?

Beat.

DR. KLEIN: Do I follow you . . . ?

GOLD: Look. You, you're under a lot of stress today, your "tragedy," I'm sorry for you. What happened to your mother. I'm going to station a man on the roof. You keep away from this side of the house. Okay?

DR. KLEIN: It's always a "fantasy." Isn't it?

GOLD: A fantasy? What's a fantasy? I don't get you.

DR. KLEIN: When someone wants to hurt the Jews.

GOLD: I've got nothing against the Jews, Doctor. I'm a Jew.

DR. KLEIN: And I'll tell you something else. When the fantasy is true, when we've been killed, then you say "what a coincidence." What a coincidence. That at the same time we were being paranoid, someone was coincidentally trying to hurt us.

GOLD *glances at* MRS. KLEIN *and then takes* DR. KLEIN *back into the kitchen.*

Interior: Kitchen—Night

GOLD: What can I have against the Jewish people, Doctor. I'm sorry, what happened to your mother. You say you saw some-one on the roof, I'm putting a man there. You tell me what more you think that I can do. (*Pause.*) Alright? *I'm Trine' a Do My Job.* (*Pause.*) I'm sorry.

DR. KLEIN: You're trying to do your job? Let's be frank, shall we?

The MAID *is still in the kitchen, and for greater privacy,* GOLD *takes* DR. KLEIN *into the alcove.*

GOLD: Sir—you wanna be frank? I don't get the whole fucken thing . . .

DR. KLEIN: It amounts to this: my mother was killed, you're assigned to the case. I called downtown, they say you're a good detective. I want *you* to find her murderer and I want protec-tion. I know you think this is a bullshit case. I don't care. You're paid to do a job. *Do* your fucken job. Have you got the pride for that?

GOLD: Don't get in my face, man.

DR. KLEIN: Have you got the pride to do the job you're given? Do your job. Or else . . .

DR. KLEIN *exits the far door of the alcove opening up into the main hall.* GOLD *follows.*

Interior: Main hall—Night

GOLD *comes out of the alcove, chasing after* DR. KLEIN.

GOLD: Don't tell me "or else." Don't tell me "or else." I'm gonna do the job. I'm not scared of your *money*. I'm not scared of *you*—I don't need your threats. I'm here to do the job.

DR. KLEIN *has proceeded up the hall toward the living room, where he joins* MRS. KLEIN *in greeting* CHAVA. *Chava's* CHAUFFEUR *is in the background.*

CHAVA: Excuse me. There was a disturbance?

GOLD *joins the group.*

GOLD: It's nothing. It's nothing to be alarmed at.

The OFFICER *is coming up the hall behind* GOLD, *and* DR. KLEIN *ushers* CHAVA *and* MRS. KLEIN *into the living room.*

OFFICER: Detective—

GOLD (*to the* OFFICER): . . . my *partner* . . . ?

OFFICER: Got to him, he says don't move, he's getting back to you, this number, ten, fifteen minutes . . .

GOLD: Okay—thanks.

GOLD *sighs. Walks to the threshold of the living room.*

The undertaker and the MAID *go their ways, and behind* GOLD, *in the living room,* KOLI, *a heavyset man, enters the front door of the apartment.*

KOLI *looks around. Two younger, very fit men follow him. They spread out.* KOLI *nods and* BENJAMIN, *an older, very well tailored distinguished man, enters, followed by another bodyguard.*

The KLEINS *and* CHAVA *are stirred by this entrance. They come over to greet* BENJAMIN, *embracing him and speaking in a foreign tongue.*

GOLD *is drawing near to this meeting.*

Gold's point of view as DR. KLEIN *motions for everyone to move to a corner sitting area.*

GOLD *watches from behind a pillar.* CHAVA *moves near to him.*

Gold's point of view: BENJAMIN *whispers to* KOLI, *pointing toward* GOLD *and* CHAVA. KOLI *walks in their direction.*

GOLD *and* CHAVA. KOLI *walks past them, and* GOLD *steps aside, placing himself right next to* CHAVA.

Their point of view: the group has drawn around BENJAMIN, *who is speaking in the foreign tongue with great feeling.*

GOLD *and* CHAVA, *who starts to cry.*

GOLD: What is he saying? You speak Hebrew?

CHAVA: It's not Hebrew. He's speaking Yiddish.

Beat.

He's . . . he says the years they spent working together, his time with her, and with . . . and with her husband, were the closest *ties* he ever had with . . . with any living being . . .

KOLI *now passes back in front of them, carrying a framed photograph, which he takes to* BENJAMIN.

Insert of the framed photograph in Benjamin's hands: a picture of two bronzed young people, dressed in khakis, at a construction site in the desert.

BENJAMIN, *speaking Yiddish, grievingly, gesturing vehemently to the picture.*

GOLD *and* CHAVA.

. . . He calls her a great woman . . . he's, he's praising her courage . . . In the years before the formation of the State of Israel, when he saw her . . .

BENJAMIN *continues speaking, tears in his eyes. He motions to one of his retainers. The retainer takes a red flyer out of his pocket, hands it to* BENJAMIN.

GOLD *and* CHAVA.

. . . now, he's talking about when they . . .

The flyer, being passed around, makes its way to GOLD *and* CHAVA. GOLD *takes it.*

GOLD *and* CHAVA.

CHAVA *becomes very attentive. Pause.*

GOLD: When they *what* . . . ?

CHAVA: It's . . . *you* know . . . it's a jargon language, Yiddish. I don't speak Yiddish that well.

CHAVA *takes leave of* GOLD, *and the* OFFICER *comes back up the hall behind him.*

OFFICER (*to* GOLD): You're wanted on the phone.

GOLD *starts down the main hall, passing the undertaker, who is coming in the opposite direction.*

Interior: The study—Night

The OFFICER *shows* GOLD *in the door, pointing to the phone on the desk.* GOLD *closes the door behind him and goes to the phone.*

GOLD: Thanks.

OFFICER: You need anything else?

GOLD: Naa, naa, just hang tight and shut the door, willya?

GOLD (*into phone*): D'tective Gold. Yeah. *Tim* . . . She . . . the old lady . . . she's goin' to give him up! She's going to give him up, you *got* her? . . . you worked her around. Fantastic. Oh, fuck *me*, why do I always miss it . . . She said *what!!!* Oh yeah. I'm the lynchpin. Big deal. Oh man, Was it sweet? I *woulda* been there, I'm stuck here with my Jews. You should see this fucken room. (*Pause.*) Naa. Fucken *bullshit*, buncha high-strung fucken *bullshit*, they pay-so-much-taxes . . . *Fuck 'em.*

Yo. She did. Fanfuckin*tastic*. What? Some bullshit, somebody's taking "shots" at them.

As GOLD *speaks, he fiddles with objects on the desk, including a magnifying glass. From this angle, Gold's body blocks
most of the view through large sliding doors into a dark
adjoining room.*

(*Into phone:*) *Fuck* 'em. Don't *tell* me, don't send the old lady
work down there, and tell me "how you're so surprised." Fuck
'em, and the taxes that they pay. (*Pause.*)

*Angle from the dark adjoining room, over a pair of hands
holding the undertaker's notebook previously seen; beyond
the notebook* GOLD *is visible through the sliding doors on
the phone in the study.*

*Reverse angle from study, with most of Gold's body blocking
the view into the adjoining room.* GOLD *leans over to reach
for another object on the desk—and reveals* MISS KLEIN
*sitting on the sofa in the next room with the notebook on
her lap.*

(*Into phone:*) You tell me. Ten more bucks a week they're
making lettin' her work down there? Not . . . "my" people,
baby . . . *Fuck* 'em, there's so much anti-Semitism, last four
thousand years, they must be doin *something* bring it about.
I'll see you at the house half hour. Yo, Tim. See you then.

*He hangs up, straightens his tie. He senses something and
looks around the room.*

Point of view: MISS KLEIN *sitting on the couch, crying
quietly, looking at him.*

Close-up: GOLD.

Close-up: MISS KLEIN.

MISS KLEIN: My grandmother was killed today.

Beat. She walks over to him.

She stayed down there because she wanted to stay there. She was a fighter. She wanted to die there. She died there.

Beat.

You're a Jew.

Beat.

And you talk that way. In the house of the dead.

Beat.

(*Softly:*) Do you have any shame?

Beat.

GOLD: I'm sorry about your grandmother.

MISS KLEIN: No one asked you to be sorry.

Beat.

No one asked for your sympathy. (*She walks to the door.*) We would have appreciated your respect.

Beat.

Do you hate yourself that much?

Beat.

Do you belong nowhere . . . ?

Beat.

GOLD: I . . .

She turns away.

I'll find the killer.

Beat.

I'll . . .

MISS KLEIN *starts out the door.* GOLD *follows.*

Interior: Main hall—Night

GOLD *chases after* MISS KLEIN.

GOLD: I swear, I'll find the killer, I swear, I . . . Listen to me, please, I . . .

Sound of a gunshot.

Close-up on MISS KLEIN, *startled.*

Close-up on GOLD, *with the* OFFICER *down the hall behind him—reaction.* GOLD *looks around.*

Interior: Living room—Night

The group around BENJAMIN *reacts to the sound.* BENJAMIN *puts the framed photograph down on a table.* KOLI *draws his gun and directs* BENJAMIN *to get against the wall. Everyone starts to exit toward the front door.*

Interior: Main hall—Night

Angle on GOLD *and the* OFFICER, *about to enter the door to the dining room.*

OFFICER: . . . it was a backfire.

GOLD *glances down the hall.*

Gold's point of view: MISS KLEIN, *terrified, pressed up against a door frame. Beyond her the group from the living room can be seen exiting the apartment.*

GOLD *and the* OFFICER. *The* OFFICER *is about to enter the dining room, and* GOLD *pushes past him.*

Interior: Dining room—Night

GOLD *rushes to the windows.*

Close-up on GOLD *looking out; the* OFFICER *is coming up behind him.*

OFFICER: Whattaya think?

GOLD: I think it's a *car* backfiring . . .

Gold's point of view out the window, panning the rooftop opposite. A few pigeons. The figure of a man standing on the roof comes into frame.

Close-up on GOLD *looking, with the* OFFICER *behind him, and* DR. KLEIN *coming in the door from the hall in the background.*

How do I get to the roof?

DR. KLEIN *points toward the kitchen.*

OFFICER: Through the kitchen. You want backup?

GOLD: No. Keep 'em out of here.

GOLD *exits the kitchen, going for the roof.*

Interior: Back service staircase—Night

GOLD *starts up the stairs two at a time.*

GOLD *climbing the stairs to a roof access door. The revolver in his hand. He puts the revolver in his coat pocket. He shoulders the door open.*

Exterior: Roofs of luxury apartment buildings—Night

GOLD *emerges onto the roof. He peers around the stairwell house.*

Point of view: the opposite roof. Nothing there.

GOLD *comes out onto the roof. Looks around behind him. Gazes down.*

Point of view: below, the police car in the street.

GOLD *on the roof. Walks toward the back of the roof.*

Point of view: the empty roof across from him.

GOLD *looks harder.*

Point of view: the shape of a man moving out from behind the stairwell house on the roof opposite.

GOLD:　Hey! Hey!

GOLD *moves in shadow to the edge of the roof. Looks down.*

Point of view: a jump of ten or twelve feet.

GOLD *jumps. His revolver falls from his pocket as he lands. He retrieves the gun and moves on.*

GOLD *moves to the stairwell house. He takes a penlight from his pocket, moves around the side of the house.*

GOLD *moving out from behind the house. Camera moves with him, settles on a bag marked* PIGEON FEED.

GOLD *rounds a corner and comes up against a pigeon coop and a boarded-up shed beyond it, the door to it just closing. A sign on the shed reads* DANGER KEEP OUT. DO NOT ENTER!!!

GOLD *takes out his gun and his flashlight. Checks the load of his gun, turns on the light. Beat. Kicks in the door, shines the light. Steps into the room.*

Interior: Shed on roof—Night

Several pigeons fly out past GOLD. *He shines his light. The room is empty.*

He stands. Beat. Looks at the DANGER KEEP OUT *sign. He kicks at the door. He lights a cigarette.*

Exterior: Roofs, continued—Night

GOLD *coming back across the roofs. Stares at the Klein's building.*

Point of view: the grandmother's room, the kitchen.

GOLD *looks down at the jump, turns back, walks to the stairwell of the building whose roof he is now on. He tugs at the roof door. The door opens. He looks down.*

Insert: the light falls upon a crumpled piece of paper lying on the roof.

GOLD *kneels, picks up the paper, smooths it open.*

Point of view: the paper on which is written, quite large, GROFAZ.

GOLD, *holding the paper. He puts it in his pocket. He turns and goes to a ladder and starts climbing back to the roof of the Klein's building.*

Interior: Main hall—Night

GOLD *joins* DR. KLEIN, MRS. KLEIN, *and* CHAVA, *and tries to reassure them.*

GOLD: No, I think everything's alright now. We've got men all over. Everything is fine.

MRS. KLEIN: There was someone on the roof . . .

DR. KLEIN: It's alright.

> DR. KLEIN *leads the two women down the hall toward the living room. From out of this group comes the* MAID *walking up the hall with the framed photograph seen previously. She hangs it back in its place on the wall near the entrance to the study.*

GOLD (*to the* MAID): Excuse me, can you think of anyone who would want to harm them . . . Did they have any enemies?

MAID: No.

GOLD: What . . . what . . . They have a lot of money. What was the old lady doing working down there?

MAID: I don't want to talk about the family.

GOLD: Just tell me that.

MAID: She made the money down there. Put the kids through school. She wanted to stay there.

> As the MAID *talks,* GOLD *glances between the photo on the wall and the windows in the dining room, which he can see through the door from the hall. He looks back at the photograph.*

GOLD: She used to work in Palestine . . .

MAID: That's right. Excuse me.

The MAID *moves off down the hall toward the living room, leaving* GOLD *alone. He is next to the photograph. It is hanging on the wall, crooked.* GOLD *straightens it. As he does so, another photograph, hidden behind the first, drops down. He removes the second photograph from behind the first.*

Insert: the same young woman. In this photo, she is holding a submachine gun and grinning.

GOLD *studies the photograph and then takes it into the study.*

Interior: Study—Night

GOLD *crosses to the desk, picks up the magnifying glass he had been fiddling with earlier, and holds it up to the photo.*

Insert: the photo, the young woman with the rifle. In the background a building with a sign over the door. The magnifying glass comes into the frame over the photo. GOLD *moves it to a box near the feet of the woman in the photograph. In magnification it is shown to be full of rifles.* GOLD *moves the glass to the sign over the door. It reads* LAUGHING PINES, ELKHART, WISCONSIN.

Exterior: Variety store street—Night

Crime scene barriers up all around.

GOLD *stands before a wall plastered with red flyers. He pulls one of the flyers off the wall.*

*Insert: the top half of the flyer. A giant rat towers over a dark cityscape—*CRIME IS CAUSED BY THE GHETTO.

GOLD *folds up the flyer and turns toward the variety store.
He comes up to a uniformed* OFFICER *stamping his feet, on
post outside the crime scene.*

OFFICER: D'tective . . .

GOLD: Yeah. How are ya'?

OFFICER: Fine, thanks. Aw'yas is colder b'fore dawn.

GOLD: Yes, I remember that.

OFFICER: You goin' in . . . ?

GOLD: Yeah.

The door to the variety store. A large sticker: CRIME SCENE.
DO NOT ENTER. *Gold's hand comes into the frame with his
flashlight, rips the sticker.*

Interior: Variety store—Night

GOLD *entering, shines his flashlight.*

GOLD: Where're the lights?

GOLD *standing by the counter, having just turned on the
light.*

GOLD *and the* OFFICER.

Interior: Variety store cellar steps—Night

*His feet on the rickety steps leading down. Thick dust, his
feet leave large footprints.*

GOLD: Valuable stuff down in the cellar?

OFFICER: That's just something they say. Something the kids been sayin' round here for years. See for yourself. Nothin's down there. Dust on the stairs. Ain't nobody been down there in years.

GOLD: Ah huh.

Interior: Variety store cellar—Night

> GOLD *coming down into the basement. He looks around.*

> *Point of view: a small room with an earthen floor. Empty cardboard boxes.* GOLD *moves into the frame. He picks up a box, looks at it. Kicks open the other boxes. They are empty.*

OFFICER (*from upstairs*): They say she kept a piece behind the counter, but what is that gonna do . . . some guy comes in with a shotgun . . . and how are you going to be watchin' the door all day, every day?

GOLD: Ah huh.

OFFICER: You can't do it. So I say I'm gonna be in here some day . . . she gets popped . . . and it was just a question of when—no more no less. I'll tell you something else. I don't know that her coming here does not make violence. A rich Jew Lady in this neighborhood is goin' to get took off. Human nature. Someday somebody gonna come in here and see what it is.

> GOLD *turns to go. He steps on a stair and it breaks.*

OFFICER: You okay down there?

GOLD: Yeah, I'm fine.

GOLD looks around, sighs. Takes a wooden box from under the stairs and upends it as a stair.

GOLD climbs up on the box.

GOLD looks down, shines his flashlight to find the step.

Point of view: the flashlight shining over the box and up on to the next step.

GOLD starts up the stairs, stops.

GOLD comes back down the stairs. Lifts the box into the light of the step so that the logo on the side of the box can be seen: AUTO-ORDINANCE COMPANY. HURLEY, N.Y.

Close-up.

He looks down at the box. GOLD *looks at the side of the box featuring the logo and the description* MANUFACTURERS OF THE TOMMY GUN . . . GOLD *opens the box.*

OFFICER: You alright down there, Detective?

Insert: the greasepaper with the AUTO-ORDINANCE *stamp on it and an exploded view of the tommy gun. He rummages to the bottom of the case and comes up with a sheet with Yiddish script written on it and a small tool kit with an instruction pamphlet* FIELD-STRIPPING THE THOMPSON GUN.

*Below that, an invoice from the Auto-Ordinance Company
for twenty tommy guns sent to a local sporting goods firm,
Kaldor Sporting Goods, 4525 Hardwick, and the date 23
August 1948. Below it is a list, penciled names of various
Jewish men.*

Interior: Police station squad room—Day

GOLD *is at his desk, his shirt open.*

*Insert: on his desk, the "Grofaz" piece of paper, the list of
names, and the tommy gun invoice. He shuffles them
around to reveal the red "Rat eating the ghetto" flyer.*

GOLD (*reading the list of names*): Hauser . . . Greenblatt . . .
Samson . . . Greenwald . . . Klein . . . Grosz . . .

The RECORDS OFFICER *enters, distributing files to various
desks.*

RECORDS OFFICER: Good morning.

GOLD: Get this to the A.T.F., will you? Good morning. And
make me copies. An invoice. Twenty Thompson guns, from
1948, and a list of names. Please run this through the com-
puter: "Grofaz."

RECORDS OFFICER: . . . grofaz . . . ?

GOLD: G.R.O.F.A.Z.

GOLD *takes a small towel and razor out of his desk. He takes
off his shirt, balls it up, and throws it into a drawer, takes*

another from out of the drawer, gets to his feet, holding the "Rat" flyer. As he does so, a UNIFORMED OFFICER *comes in and addresses the* GROUNDER, *who is in the holding cell.*

RECORDS OFFICER: What is it, a name?

GOLD: I dunno what it is.

RECORDS OFFICER: Alright. Have a good day.

UNIFORMED OFFICER (*to the* GROUNDER): Get up. Taking you in for arraignment, Mr. Wells.

GOLD *proceeds back to the washbasin, the* UNIFORMED OFFICER *follows.*

D'tective . . . ?

GOLD: Yeah.

UNIFORMED OFFICER: . . . need you to file a *complaint* on this man.

GOLD: A complaint . . . ?

UNIFORMED OFFICER (*checks his notepad*): Uh . . . he *assaulted* you.

GOLD: Forget it.

UNIFORMED OFFICER: Assault, police officer, attempted escape.

GOLD: Yeah. *Forget* it. The fucken guy. He shot his wife and

kids, now whadda they gonna . do to him for beating on
me . . . ?

UNIFORMED OFFICER: Sir, the thing is, you need to mak'n
example, the guy, hittin' on a *cop*.

GOLD: Hey, leave it, alright . . . ?

GROUNDER: I won't forget this, Officer. *Thank* you. I'll make it
up to you. I *promise*.

GOLD: . . . you're gonna make it up to me?

GROUNDER: Yes. I will. Your kindness has changed my life.

GOLD: Well, that's swell.

GROUNDER: And someday I'll repay you.

At the washbasin, GOLD *sticks the red "Rat eating the
ghetto" flyer behind the mirror. We now see the entire cap-
tion, which reads* CRIME IS CAUSED BY THE GHETTO, THE
GHETTO IS CAUSED BY THE JEW! *The rat wears a yarmulke.*

GOLD: Uh-huh. My thoughts are elsewhere. You must par-
don me.

GOLD *goes back to his desk, puts on his new shirt, and sits at
his desk staring at the "Rat" flyer. The* GROUNDER *is led out
of the cell by the* UNIFORMED OFFICER.

Lap dissolve: GOLD *sitting at his desk, afternoon, various
foodstuff wrappings around him. He is on the phone.*

Yeah, "Grofaz." G.R.O.F.A.Z.

A delivery boy drops a sandwich on Gold's desk.

How ya doin', Billy—

BILLY: You all alone here today?

GOLD: Yeah, I'm never goin' home. Here. Keep it.

BILLY: Thanks.

GOLD (*on the phone*): . . . anything you might have. Particularly anything connected with anti-Jewish acts . . . Well, if you do, will you please call me here. Thank you.

He hangs up the phone.

RANDOLPH'S MOTHER: That's him. That's the man.

Gold looks up.

Gold's point of view: RANDOLPH'S MOTHER *being led into the squadroom by* FRANK, OLCOTT, *and* CURRAN.

That's him. That's the man. You the one. I'm going to *do* it, but I'm goin' to do it with *you. You* going to take him in. Like you told me. Nice and gentle. No harm come to him. You *swore* that . . .

She is led into the interrogation room by FRANK *and* OLCOTT. CURRAN *stays behind and perches on Gold's desk.*

CURRAN: Well, you won her around, man.

GOLD: I did?

CURRAN: You said the magic word, the duck came down. Five a.m., Randolph meets his mother. Here's the setup: she's gonna get him out of the country. Get him a ticket.

FRANK (*from the interrogation room*): Jilly, you want to come in here?

CURRAN: Hold it a minute, Frank. We have her tell Randolph she'll get the passport of a *friend* of his . . . (*Hands photo to* GOLD.) So: Randolph thinks he's gonna take the passport and go to South America. We have his mom make a date with him . . .

GOLD: Jilly . . . I got to work on this thing here . . .

CURRAN: No, Bob, the broad won't show unless you're there, you're the man going to bring him in. Five a.m., tomorrow . . .

GOLD: I got to work on this thing . . .

CURRAN: . . . put it on the shelf.

GOLD: I can't.

CURRAN: You got to. We're taking Randolph five a.m. Tomorrow you're gonna be there. Get over the passport office, right now. Sully's waiting for you. Give 'em these pictures. This is the big one, Bob.

FRANK (*offscreen*): Jilly . . .

CURRAN: I'm coming, Frank . . . Get over to the passport office right now.

Interior: Passport office—Day

Insert: the sheet of paper bearing the word GROFAZ, *and the other clues, spread out on a desk.*

The passport office, SULLIVAN *at the counter, walks back to a bench. Camera pans him there. Seated at the bench is* GOLD, *looking at the "Grofaz" piece of paper.* SULLIVAN *sits.*

SULLIVAN: This rendezvous with Randolph takes place at five a.m. at . . . (*Pause.*) Bob . . . ? (*Pause.*)

GOLD: I was out all night on this. Now. Tell me what you make of this. I got a *picture* of this woman, taken in Wisconsin. Nice old Jewish woman, with a tommy gun. Alright? What is she doing with an *invoice* for these tommy guns, the basement? I got a . . . last night . . . I got Israeli Heavy Hitters coming in, I've got some guy on the *roof* . . . I . . .

SULLIVAN: Yes. It's a "myster" . . . innit . . . ?

GOLD (*passing him a photograph*): Look: this is taken in *Wisconsin.* 1946 . . .

SULLIVAN: Bob. Hey, *Bob* . . . hey. Get *out* of it. We've got a *job* to do. *Tonight* the balloon goes up. The *old* days, Bobby, huh? You bust a case, bottle comes out, you stick your feet on the filing cabinet, hey? We lure Randolph out and we take him in. You got it? Third and Racine, you got it?

GOLD: . . . this other case.

SULLIVAN: Fuck the other case . . . *what* other case? What other case?

GOLD: This, this Jewish . . .

SULLIVAN: It's a candy store pop? Just look busy on it.

GOLD: I, I, you know, I *caught* the case.

SULLIVAN (*pause*): What is there, a *broad* in it?

Draws him closer.

What is the *thing?*

GOLD: It's just, I think it's some sort of conspiracy . . .

SULLIVAN: Some sort of conspiracy?

GOLD: They said someone was shooting at them . . .

SULLIVAN: Someone was shooting at them, the Jew family . . .

GOLD: Yes.

SULLIVAN: . . . and *was* there someone shooting at them, hmm, Bob . . . ?

Beat.

SULLIVAN moves over to GOLD and cups his face in his hand.

Tight on the two.

Hey? You got some heavy troubles on your mind? Baby? We'll work it out. We'll play some cops and robbers, we'll bust this *Big Criminal*, we'll swagger *around* . . . huh?

Beat.

GOLD: You're like my family, Tim.

SULLIVAN: Bob . . . I *am* your family . . .

CLERK (*voice-over*): Here you go.

They look up. The CLERK *is holding an envelope.*

One passport. "Show and Tell."

The CLERK *hands an envelope to* SULLIVAN, *who takes the passport from the envelope.*

Insert: the envelope is stamped FORGED DOCUMENT OFFICIAL USE ONLY.

I will require your signature on these documents and these also require your star number, may I see it please? Please fill in only those sections marked as required. This is a release form, please read it. All of these documents remain the property of the passport office and are loaned to you only for the purposes set forward in your application.

SULLIVAN: Third and Racine.

SULLIVAN turns the envelope over and writes "Third and Racine, 5 a.m." on the back.

CLERK: Your acceptance of them constitutes a release of responsibility for this office . . .

SULLIVAN: Five a.m.

GOLD: Third and Racine.

GOLD *starts to take out a cigarette.*

CLERK: . . . until they are returned to our physical custody. Misuse of or malfeasance in regard to this document is a federal crime. I'm sorry. You can't smoke in here.

SULLIVAN: Meet you in the hall.

GOLD *nods. Starts out into the hall.*

CLERK: Now we have the G-22-A.

Interior: Corridor outside Bureau of Alcohol, Tobacco and Firearms—Day

GOLD *stands in the hallway. Two men are coming out of the room.*

FIRST OFFICER: Okay. I'll file the forms and I'll see you tomorrow morning.

SECOND OFFICER: Okay.

FIRST OFFICER: Thanks a lot. A-1.

SECOND OFFICER: Sure thing. Going up to the country this weekend?

FIRST OFFICER: No, I'm staying in town. Seeya later.

GOLD *pauses a moment and enters the Bureau.*

Interior: Federal building elevator—Day

RICK *and* JERRY *talking in elevator.*

JERRY: I *rebel* . . .

Elevator bell sounds as doors open.

RICK: Jerry . . .

JERRY: . . . wait a second. I *rebel* any time somebody tells me . . .

RICK *and* JERRY *exit as* GOLD *and* SULLIVAN *enter elevator;* GOLD *is holding the Xerox of the tommy gun invoice.*

GOLD: I just saw the A.T.F.; they were stolen, Sully. The tommy guns were *stolen* . . . all the guns on the invoice . . .

SULLIVAN: Hey, you're better than an aquarium, you know, there's something happening with you every minute . . .

GOLD: What does it *mean?*

SULLIVAN: It don't mean *nothing*. Some broad got killed. She's *dead* now . . . Okay. You're goin' to the ticket office, pick up Randolph's ticket . . . This is the big one, Laddie.

GOLD: Timmy, this other case . . .

SULLIVAN: Bob.

GOLD: I got this piece of paper I found, *"Grofaz."*

He hands the paper and the holster strap to SULLIVAN.

SULLIVAN: "Grofaz." What does it mean?

GOLD: I don't *know* what it means, but I got this fella on the roof. At the Jewish house . . .

SULLIVAN: What was he doing? Shooting at them . . . ?

GOLD: I don't know.

SULLIVAN: Well, then *drop* it. Bobby. For Chrissake. I don't get it.

GOLD: Maybe you don't want to get it.

SULLIVAN: What do you mean?

GOLD: Nothing.

SULLIVAN: What do you mean? 'Cause I ain't a Yid.

Beat.

GOLD: Well, you ain't a Yid.

SULLIVAN: And so, what? I'm an anti-Semite . . . ? What the fuck are you saying?

GOLD: It's just not your thing, Tim. It's not your thing, it's my thing, okay?

SULLIVAN: Bob. I want to tell you what the Old Whore said—and this is the truest thing I know—When you start coming with the customers, it's time to quit. What is this . . . ?

GOLD: It's the strap the guy tore off my holster.

SULLIVAN: Well. Go and get it fixed, will you? Go take a cooling walk, something.

GOLD: You mad at me?

SULLIVAN: Yeah, I'm mad at you. I'm not going to invite you to my birthday party, you dumb kike. Go get your holster fixed.

Exterior: Street outside shoe repair store—Day

   GOLD *coming up to the shoe repair store. The owner is closing the grate; he is an older Jewish man.*

GOLD: Excuse me.

SHOEMAKER: We're closed.

GOLD: Well. I wonder, could you help me?

SHOEMAKER: We're closed. We're closing.

GOLD: I just need, I got a little problem . . .

   He flashes his holster.

I'm a police officer, I lost the *strap* offa my *holster* . . .

SHOEMAKER: . . . I can't, I'm closing up . . . I'm sorry . . .

GOLD *nods.* GOLD *steps into the alcove of the shop, while the* SHOEMAKER *closes up.*

SHOEMAKER: . . . you're a *policeman* . . .

GOLD: Yes.

SHOEMAKER: Show it to me . . .

GOLD *takes his holster off of his belt and hands it to the shoemaker. Puts his revolver in his suit coat pocket.*

GOLD *digs in his pocket.*

Insert: the strap, in his pocket, wrapped in a piece of paper.

He hands the strap and paper to the shoemaker.

He opens the paper.

Close-up: the SHOEMAKER *looking at the paper.*

GOLD: What is it?

SHOEMAKER: The word.

He hands the strap back to GOLD, *then the paper.*

Insert: the paper, held by GOLD. *The word* GROFAZ.

GOLD: The word. You know what the word means . . . ?

SHOEMAKER: Yes. I know what it means.

He continues closing the heavy grate and locks it.

It means Hitler. It was another name they had for Hitler.

The SHOEMAKER *turns up his collar, goes out into the rain.*

Interior: Library—Day

A *blackboard, a man's hand. On it is written* GRÖSSTER FELDHERR ALLER ZEITEN.

LIBRARIAN (*voice-over*): Grösster.

He underlines GRÖ *from* GRÖSSTER.

Feldherre.

He underlines F *from* FELDHERR.

Aller.

He underlines the A *from* ALLER.

Zeiten.

He underlines the Z *from* ZEITEN.

Angle: the LIBRARIAN, *at the board. A young Jewish man in a suit wearing a yarmulke.*

"Grösster Feldherr aller Zeiten," the greatest . . . strategist . . . of all time. Der Grofaz.

He walks back to the poster of Hitler and gestures to it.

Hitler.

The LIBRARIAN *opens a file to reveal a huge colored poster of Hitler in a trench with German soldiers. Hitler is pointing to a map, while the Germans listen, awestruck. Across the bottom of the poster is written* DER GROFAZ.

Are you alright?

Gold's hand with the sheet of paper with GROFAZ *on it.*

GOLD: No, I, ah, I just didn't get much sleep last night.

LIBRARIAN (*voice-over*): You know, you have a very interesting request. The acronym is not well known.

The LIBRARIAN *takes Gold's arm and escorts him through a gallery filled with Nazi posters.*

It was used at the *end* of the war. The name is obviously the effort of their propaganda ministry. It was an interesting attempt, but it didn't particularly "take" . . . but it *was* used . . . it *was* used . . .

He leads GOLD *to a filing cabinet.*

By the group . . . the . . .

He finds the piece of paper he is looking for.

Sonderkommando . . . it was adopted by the Sonderendlösungkommando of the Division Leibstandarte Adolph Hitler . . . That is, the special group for the Final Solution, which is, of course, the extermination of the Jews . . .

He hands a German leaflet to GOLD.

Insert: GOLD *holding the leaflet with the word* GROFAZ *fairly large.*

The LIBRARIAN *and* GOLD. *The* LIBRARIAN *translates.*

"German people, follow the Grofaz. Leibstandarte Adolph Hitler fights on all fronts for the salvation of Germany. The Jewish scourge can be cleansed only in blood . . ." *(To* GOLD:) This is a *very* rare piece . . .

GOLD: What do you have on the use of this word? Currently? Particularly, in conjunction with . . . with anti-Semitic acts.

LIBRARIAN: As I said, it's an arcane usage . . . but we'll look . . .

He calls to an ASSISTANT.

in the current anti-Semitism under *Grofaz,* cross-referenced *der Führer,* bring it all.

The ASSISTANT *moves off. The* LIBRARIAN *gestures* GOLD *to follow him.*

. . . if you'd care to wait . . .

GOLD *moves to the water fountain.*

At the water fountain GOLD *sweeps back his jacket to get to a handkerchief in his back pocket. The jacket catches on the butt of his revolver and stays open, revealing his revolver and his shield, which is on the belt in front of it.* GOLD *wets the handkerchief and applies it to his head.*

Close-up: GOLD *holding the handkerchief to his head. He feels someone looking at him. He turns.*

Point of view: in the room beyond, a young Chasidic SCHOLAR *with books spread out on the table in front of him is staring at* GOLD. GOLD *walks into his point of view and over to him.*

The SCHOLAR *and* GOLD.

GOLD: I'm a police officer.

Beat.

The revolver disturbs you. The gun disturbs you? I'm a police officer.

SCHOLAR: The gun doesn't disturb me.

GOLD: You were looking at me.

SCHOLAR: The gun is nothing. The gun is a tool. We have nothing to fear from a tool. The *badge* concerns me, you see . . . the badge is a *symbol* . . .

A LIBRARY WORKER *comes into the room.*

The SCHOLAR *nods, stands—using a cane. He calls* GOLD
over to his side of the table.

The *badge,* you see, is the *symbol.* Of that which constrains us.

*He gestures at the table. Amid various manuscripts is a
notebook in which the* SCHOLAR *has drawn a six-pointed star
and, below it, a five-pointed star. The tablet is covered in
mathematical symbols and in Hebrew script.*

SCHOLAR: The *star . . .* you see. The star. The five-point star.
The *pentagram . . .* it is identified as a star, but it is not the
symbol of heaven. It is the symbol of *earth . . .* The Mogen
David (*he gestures to the six-pointed star*) is the intersection of
the opposites and can be deconstructed into heaven and earth,
but the pentagram cannot be deconstructed. You see? The five
points are the five senses, the Chinese five elements, the five
fingers of the hand. You see? You're Jewish . . . ? Are you
Jewish?

GOLD: . . . yes.

SCHOLAR: Well. You see? (*He gestures to one of the books.*)
From the Book of Esther.

GOLD *and the* SCHOLAR. GOLD *still looking down.*

"Esther." From "Sathar," to *conceal.* But what is concealed?
What is *concealed?* In the name "Esther"? And the answer is
here. Here is the answer—

He gestures at one of his books.

Do you see . . . ?

GOLD *looks down.*

Insert: the Hebrew text.

GOLD: . . . I can't read it.

Beat.

SCHOLAR: You say you're a Jew?

GOLD: I can't read it.

The LIBRARY WORKER *comes back in.*

The SCHOLAR *starts gathering his materials together.*

SCHOLAR: You say you're a Jew and you can't read Hebrew? What *are* you then . . . ?

The SCHOLAR *starts out of the room, carrying several large books. He calls back to* GOLD.

Would you get that book for me?

GOLD *is left with a large volume that the* SCHOLAR *has left behind. He looks down at it.*

Insert: the volume, covered in Cabalistic symbols and Hebrew text.

GOLD *picks up the volume, starts after the* SCHOLAR, *who goes through the stacks.*

(*Over his shoulder:*) Would you replace the book for me please . . . It goes up there.

The SCHOLAR *gestures to an open spot on the stacks.*

GOLD *goes up the ladder to replace the book.*

ASSISTANT LIBRARIAN (*voice-over*): . . . the material on anti-Semitic acts . . .

LIBRARIAN (*voice-over*): Yes, I thought that we had quite a file of current . . .

GOLD *looks through the space created by the book he is about to replace.*

Point of view: through the space in the bookshelf. The two LIBRARIANS.

ASSISTANT LIBRARIAN: . . . it was requested by Two Twelve.

LIBRARIAN: . . . Two Twelve wants it . . . ?

ASSISTANT LIBRARIAN: Yes.

LIBRARIAN: Well, it's a "Two Twelve" now. Fine, then just pull the file.

ASSISTANT LIBRARIAN: Okay.

LIBRARIAN: Thanks.

The ASSISTANT LIBRARIAN *walks away.*

GOLD *on the ladder. He replaces the book and starts down the ladder. He walks back to the table where he met the scholar. The* LIBRARIAN *walks over to him.*

The material on anti-Semitic acts—. . . no, we have nothing on that.

GOLD: Nothing?

LIBRARIAN: No.

GOLD: This is official police business.

LIBRARIAN: Officer, you know I'd help you if I could, but as I said. It was rather arcane material . . . I'm sorry.

GOLD: Well, if there's nothing you can do, there's nothing you can do . . . thank you.

LIBRARIAN: Not at all. If there's anything else I can help you with, let me know.

GOLD *looks down at the clipboard that the* LIBRARIAN *has been given by his* ASSISTANT.

Insert: extreme close-up—on the bottom of the clipboard a piece of stationery with the address "212 Humboldt Street."

Exterior: Deserted schoolhouse—Night

Point of view: set in the stones of a deserted schoolhouse, a small mosaic number plate reads "212."

GOLD, *looking at the number plate, looks up the steps.*

The boarded-up front of the deserted schoolhouse.

GOLD *starts around the side of the building. Camera pans with him. Camera follows* GOLD *alongside the building to a small side door that is bolted.*

GOLD *is attempting to lever open the side door to 212. He hears something.*

Close-up: GOLD, *looking toward the source of the sound.*

Point of view: a YOUNG COUPLE, *walking their Doberman, are stopped and looking at him.*

GOLD *walks over to the young couple.*

GOLD: . . . I . . . can you tell me anything about this building?

YOUNG MAN: What?

GOLD: Do you know anything about this building?

YOUNG WOMAN: . . . no . . .

They back away from him.

GOLD: . . . I just . . .

YOUNG WOMAN: . . . about the building . . . ?

GOLD: Yes.

YOUNG MAN: Do you live around here . . . ?

GOLD: Please, just tell me. Have you ever seen anyone come in or out . . . ?

The YOUNG MAN *and the* YOUNG WOMAN *see something.*

YOUNG MAN (*in Hebrew*): He has a gun . . .

Angle on the YOUNG COUPLE. *The* YOUNG WOMAN *pulls a gun from the young man's shirt. Beyond them the* CHAUFFEUR *and a group of several men walk up to the fence.*

YOUNG MAN: Against the fence. Get against the fence and grab it.

YOUNG WOMAN: Get up against the fence.

GOLD *moves to the fence. The* YOUNG WOMAN *holds the gun on him.*

YOUNG WOMAN: Now grab the fence or I will shoot you dead.

He looks around, confused. The CHAUFFEUR *detaches himself from the group of men and walks to the fence.*

CHAUFFEUR (*in Hebrew, to the* YOUNG COUPLE): He's a police officer. (*To* GOLD, *in English:*) What brings you out this evening?

Beat.

Mr. Gold?

GOLD: I want to know about the old woman.

CHAUFFEUR: We know nothing.

GOLD: I think she was involved in running guns.

CHAUFFEUR: . . . running guns . . . ?

GOLD: Long ago.

CHAUFFEUR: Why's that?

GOLD: . . . and I found a list. A list of Jewish names. Men. Here. In this city . . . I think they were running guns with her. I . . .

BENJAMIN *steps forward from the group of men.*

CHAUFFEUR: How did you get this address? What are you doing here?

BENJAMIN: Why are you here?

GOLD: I need help. I want to know why she was killed.

Beat.

BENJAMIN *gestures. The door to the abandoned schoolhouse opens.* BENJAMIN *looks at* GOLD.

BENJAMIN: Alright.

Interior: Deserted schoolhouse—Night

The group enters. Camera travels with them into the school kitchen, where several hefty young men who were present at the shiva at Klein's apartment are sitting around. The group from the alley comes in.

BENJAMIN: This way, Mr. Gold. Please sit down.

> BENJAMIN *and* KOLI *take off their jackets.* KOLI *wears a German semiautomatic pistol in a shoulder holster. One of the* YOUNG MEN *brings coffee in white Navy mugs, puts them in front of all.*

> *The* YOUNG BODYGUARD *shrugs. Moves off.*

> BENJAMIN *indicates the pistol in Koli's holster.*

You see that gun? I had one . . . just like it. I gave mine to that kid in Hebron. Last year. Two years ago . . . ?

> KOLI *shrugs.*

They told me that it was an affectation. For me to still wear the gun.

> *Beat.*

But you get *used* to it. You know . . . ? (*Sighs.*) Eh, Koli . . . ?

KOLI: That's right.

BENJAMIN (*to* GOLD): Would you like something to eat, Mr. Gold? I'm going to have something to eat. (*To the man from the shiva:*) Barry, you want something . . . ?

BARRY: Sure, love to.

KOLI: They shot the old lady.

BARRY: I know.

BENJAMIN (*to* GOLD): Barry was with us in the old days. And Bert, and Marv—

BARRY: That's right.

BENJAMIN: What a time that was. Mr. Gold. What a woman she was.

Beat.

GOLD: I want to find the men who killed her.

BENJAMIN: Yes. And we need your help.

GOLD: You have it.

BENJAMIN (*nodding*): Yes.

GOLD: She was running guns. (*Beat.*) Wasn't she?

Beat.

BENJAMIN: Yes. During our War of Independence. In our country, we call her a hero.

Beat.

GOLD: And . . . why would anyone want to kill her *now* . . . ?

BENJAMIN: I don't know. But we must find *out*. So many of us. Good Americans. Good Jews. Who are good friends to Israel. We always need such friends, you know?

MARV: Isn't that the truth . . .

GOLD: . . . yes.

BENJAMIN: You . . . you are such a man.

GOLD: I . . . ?

Beat.

BENJAMIN: You'd like . . . to fight. For your home.

GOLD: I would do anything.

BENJAMIN *gestures to the group as if to say "As I foretold, he is one of us."* BENJAMIN *leans over and kisses* GOLD *on the cheek. He moves his chair closer.*

BENJAMIN: Now—we are going to *find* her killers. We are going to *find* them and to *deal* with them. You mention a list. Now—we need it.

GOLD *hands the photocopy to* BENJAMIN.

No. The original.

GOLD: It's at the precinct house.

BENJAMIN (*nods*): Good. Bring it with you. When you next come.

He gestures to the CHAUFFEUR.

Asher will fill you in on what we've . . .

GOLD: No, I can't bring, excuse me, I can't bring the *original* . . .

BENJAMIN (*explaining*): No, that's what we need. You see. That's the *evidence*. It *must* be . . . it *must* be . . . it must be destroyed. It cannot come to light. She was killed. (*Gestures to* BARRY.) This man, good men in this city. If that list came to light. You see. They are in *danger.*

GOLD: But, but . . .

BENJAMIN: . . . yes . . . ?

GOLD: . . . the list is evidence. I've logged it, into an evidence bag.

Beat.

I've . . . I've signed it in. I . . . I can't take thhh . . . it's evidence . . . Please, you know, *anything,* I . . .

BENJAMIN: No, not "anything," the *list* is what I need.

GOLD: Anything else, I . . .

BENJAMIN: Yes, yes, anything else. Of course.

BENJAMIN *writes Hebrew characters on the blackboard.*

BENJAMIN: That is your name in Hebrew. Are you a Jew, Mr. Gold?

GOLD: Yes.

BENJAMIN (*nods*): Then be a Jew! You can't take that list. How long your resolution lasts. Until the first unpleasantness.

GOLD: . . . I am a sworn Police Officer, I . . .

BENJAMIN: WHERE ARE YOUR LOYALTIES? You want the Glory, you want the *Home*, you are willing to do *nothing* . . .

GOLD: I . . . I took an oath . . .

BENJAMIN (*in Hebrew*): You took an oath! He disgusts me. Get him out of here.

He is escorted to the door by the bodyguards.

Exterior: Alley, outside the deserted schoolhouse—Night

YOUNG BODYGUARD (*as he ejects* GOLD): . . . don't bother to return. The next time you come, there will be nobody here . . .

The door closes.

GOLD *in the alley, looking toward the street.*

Point of view: a car is stopped. The LIBRARIAN *gets out of the car, looking for something.*

GOLD *moves down the alley. Hides himself somewhat.*

Exterior: Deserted schoolhouse—Night

Gold's point of view: CHAVA *coming down the steps of the 212 building, goes over to the* LIBRARIAN, *who hands her the anti-Semitic flyer and talks for a moment to her. She thanks him. The* LIBRARIAN *gets back into the car and drives off. Beat.* CHAVA *checks her watch, glances at the pamphlet, and puts it in her purse. She goes to a car parked down the street.*

Unlocking the car, CHAVA *gets in. Puts the pamphlet on the dashboard. Looks up.*

Point of view: GOLD *standing by her.*

The two of them.

CHAVA: Yes?

GOLD: I need . . . I need to *help* . . .

CHAVA: In what way?

GOLD: I want to *help* you. In your work.

CHAVA: I work for the *airlines* . . .

GOLD: Please. Please. Let me help. With whatever you do.

CHAVA: What I do, Mr. Gold, you don't want to know.

GOLD: No, but I *do*. I *need* to . . . please . . . please . . . whatever you're doing. What you're doing tonight. Let me help. Please. (*Beat.*) I'm begging you.

   Beat.

Please.

   Beat.

Close-up: CHAVA.

Hold.

Interior: Diner—Night

A *small sleazy roadside diner.* GOLD *and* CHAVA *sitting across from each other.* GOLD *is talking. He is high.*

GOLD: What can I tell you about it. They said . . . I was a *pussy* all my life. They said I was a pussy, because I was a Jew. Onna' cops, they'd say, send a Jew, mizewell send a *broad* on the job, send a *broad* through the door . . . All my goddamned life, and I listened to it . . . uh-huh . . . ? I was the donkey . . . I was the "clown" . . .

CHAVA: . . . you were the Outsider.

GOLD: . . . yes . . .

CHAVA: . . . I understand.

GOLD: They made me the hostage negotiator, 'cause I knew how the bad guys felt.

CHAVA: Doing Other People's Work for them . . .

GOLD: . . . that's right.

CHAVA: . . . in their country . . .

GOLD: Yes, that's right.

CHAVA: . . . and never working for yourself.

GOLD: Yes. Now—why would I do that?

> *Beat.*

You have your *own* home.

CHAVA: Yes. I do.

GOLD: Now—what can that be like?

> *Beat.*

To have your own country?

> CHAVA *sighs.*

CHAVA: I'm gone so much of the time.

> *Beat.*

But I think about it.

> GOLD *nods his head, slowly.*
>
> *Close-up:* CHAVA.
>
> *Close-up:* GOLD *looking at her.*
>
> *Close-up:* CHAVA.

(*Softly:*) I know.

GOLD: I sat with those *guys* tonight . . . with *heroes* . . . Jewish guys who had Nothing To Prove. And I felt . . . I felt, Jesus, all my life, I got to be . . . the first one in the door . . . and . . . huh? Not for *me, all for someone else* . . . Why? Because *I was no good.* Because I'm nobody. I want to be a part of it, that's all.

Exterior: Model train store—Night

   A small suburban street. The car. CHAVA *and* GOLD *in the car.*

Interior: Chava's car—Night

   CHAVA *pulls out the "Rat eating the ghetto" flyer.*

CHAVA: We think this leaflet was printed at that shop. The shop is owned by Mr. Andersen, who is head of a group called the United Action Front, who, we think, may have had something to do with the murder of Mrs. Klein.

GOLD: And what were you sent here to do?

CHAVA: To find out if the leaflet was printed there.

GOLD: . . . and if it was . . . ?

CHAVA: . . . if it was, then I'm going to give them a message.

   She picks up a black box and starts to get out of the car.

CHAVA: . . . I won't be long.

GOLD: Let me do it for you.

CHAVA: No. I can't do that. Wait—

GOLD *takes the black box, starts out of the car.*

CHAVA: Give that back to me. Give it back.

Exterior: Model train store—Night

CHAVA *follows* GOLD *out of the car and comes around to meet him.*

CHAVA: I can't let you do it.

GOLD: I'm going. How do I get in? I'm going. If I don't go nobody's going. How do I get in?

CHAVA: Alright, then.

She hands him a small kit of lockpicks.

CHAVA: Can you use these lockpicks . . . ?

GOLD: Yes.

CHAVA (*referring to the box*): Can you use that? The bottom button, then the top.

GOLD *nods. Beat. He starts across the street.*

GOLD *walking around the corner of the model train store. The sign* ANDERSEN'S MODEL TRAIN STORE *seen large in the frame.* GOLD *walks around to the door, takes out a set of lockpicks, and picks the lock.*

Interior: Andersen's model train store—Night

GOLD, *entering, shuts the door behind him. Walks to a table, illuminated by the streetlamp shining in the window.*

Point of view: GOLD *looks around the store.*

GOLD, *walking over to the window, looks out.*

He walks through the store, passing a glass cabinet with a miniature town set up inside. He passes glass cases filled with toy soldiers and policemen and stops to look at them.

He sees the stockroom and walks to it. He sets the bomb down and opens the door. There is nothing inside and he closes the door. He hears a noise and, opening the door again, discovers a brown shirt on the floor. Lifting the shirt to look at it closely, he sees a swastika on the arm.

He goes inside the stockroom and shuts the door.

Interior: Stockroom—Night

Inside the stockroom he discovers another room with a small printing press.

Above the printing press hangs a large Nazi swastika flag.

GOLD *moves past the printing press and sees a photograph on the wall.*

Insert: the photo. Dead bodies next to a mass grave. Laughing storm troopers standing above them. A mother clutches her child.

Along the wall is a table full of anti-Semitic literature, including a freshly printed newsletter.

GOLD *picks up a copy of the newsletter.*

Insert: THE AMERICAN CHRISTIAN SENTINEL.

> *It Is Only Common Sense To Cull The Weak.*
> *The admixture of Jewish blood into the clan's White Race is a crime against humanity, against which the greatest plagues of history must pale.*
> *The effeminate ideals and weak appearance of the Jew, proclaims to all their inferiority.*
> *To tolerate the presence of this vile sickness in our midst is not justice, IT IS MADNESS.*

Interior: Model train store—Night

GOLD *comes out of the stockroom reading the newsletter. He wipes his brow. He puts down the paper and, picking up an engine, smashes the toy town case.*

GOLD *picks up the black box he carried from the car. He opens the box.*

Insert: the device. He turns the dial. Pushes a button to activate the bomb.

GOLD, *putting the device down on a small printing press.*

Exterior: Model train store—Night

GOLD, *coming out of the door, around the "Andersen's*

Model Train Store" sign. He comes toward the camera as the building behind him explodes into flames.

The car, CHAVA sitting in the driver's seat. GOLD gets into the passenger seat and the car drives off.

Interior: Diner—Night

Point of view: the CHAUFFEUR and one of his associates enter the diner.

GOLD and CHAVA. He looks to her, then toward the door.

The CHAUFFEUR and his men. Camera brings them to the booth. The CHAUFFEUR sits. Beat. He looks questioningly at CHAVA.

CHAVA: We went to that place.

The CHAUFFEUR nods.

CHAUFFEUR: Good.

GOLD: I want to be a part of it.

The CHAUFFEUR nods.

CHAUFFEUR: Good. Then you are a part of it. You've *shown* it. And now we need something from you.

GOLD: Yes.

CHAUFFEUR: That list. Of names. We need the list.

Beat.

GOLD: I've told you. As a policeman, I can't . . .

CHAUFFEUR: . . . we need it.

CHAVA: What he wants. Give it to him, please . . .

GOLD: I've explained it to him. I can't. It's evidence. Why, why, do you want me to "prove" myself to . . . haven't I done that tonight?

CHAUFFEUR: We don't want you to prove yourself—we want that list.

GOLD: No. I told you.

Beat.

The CHAUFFEUR. *He looks up.*

Point of view: behind him, a YOUNG MAN *from 212 Humboldt Street entering the diner, holding a manila envelope.*

GOLD *turns to look at the* YOUNG MAN, *who hands the envelope to the* CHAUFFEUR. *He takes out several photographs and spreads them on the table. The* YOUNG MAN *takes the briefcase and goes to the front of the diner.*

CHAUFFEUR (*in English*): I'm sorry . . . The building you entered was under surveillance, here are some photographs of you entering and leaving.

He gestures to the photographs.

Insert: the photos: GOLD *breaking into the train store.* GOLD *leaving the building—in flames.*

GOLD *and the* CHAUFFEUR. *The* CHAUFFEUR *takes the photos of* GOLD *breaking in and slips them into Gold's shirt pocket.*

CHAUFFEUR: *Look at them at your leisure. We need the list.*

Close-up: GOLD *looks at* CHAVA.

Point of view: CHAVA *looks away.*

GOLD *and the* CHAUFFEUR.

GOLD *turns to look at* CHAVA, *who is leaving the booth.*

Close-up: GOLD *looking on.*

GOLD *turns, begins to hit the* CHAUFFEUR *in the face; the* CHAUFFEUR *hits him in the stomach.*

The YOUNG MAN *comes to the aid of the* CHAUFFEUR. *The* CHAUFFEUR *rises to his feet.*

CHAUFFEUR (*in Hebrew*): It's alright . . . it's alright . . . *out* . . .

The CHAUFFEUR *and the* YOUNG MAN *back out of the diner.*

Close-up: GOLD *looking toward the door.*

Point of view: CHAVA *is the last to depart, gives him one last look.*

GOLD *standing stunned in the middle of the floor. He draws out the photos from his shirt pocket.*

Insert: the photos of him breaking into the building. Among the photos he finds the passport envelope, which says FORGED DOCUMENT OFFICIAL USE ONLY. *He turns over the envelope and sees "Third and Racine, 5:00 a.m."*

Close-up: GOLD *looks at his watch.*

Insert: the watch reads 5:03.

Close-up: GOLD.

GOLD: . . . Oh, my God . . .

Exterior: Ghetto street—Night

GOLD *running. Camera dollies with him.*

Wide angle showing GOLD *approaching a corner. He slows down.*

GOLD *adjusts his breathing. Starts to come around the corner.*

Close-up: GOLD *looking around; he hears a shot and runs toward the sound.*

Exterior: Abandoned building—Night

GOLD *runs alongside the wall from the corner of Third and*

Racine. He comes upon SENNA *and* OLCOTT *crouched behind a car.* SENNA *is on the walkie.*

SENNA: I got a man down. I need an ambulance *right now.*

Shots are fired at the car. OLCOTT *returns fire.*

OLCOTT (*to* GOLD): Where were you?

GOLD: What happened? What went down . . . ?

OLCOTT: The whole thing's gone down.

SENNA (*to walkie*): Sully. Pull out. PULL OUT!!! Leave 'em up there . . . Let S.W.A.T. take 'em.

A car pulls up behind them. SENNA *turns to them as* OLCOTT *fires again.*

(*To the arriving officers:*) You guys, take cover, stay tight to the wall.

BATES (*on the radio*): I got the uniform kid hit bad.

SENNA (*to walkie*): Bring 'em down, bring 'em down, I got an ambulance coming in.

GOLD *and* OLCOTT *fire at the window.*

Sullivan, Frank. You two, get the hell out of there . . .

RADIO (*approaching patrol car*): I'm coming in west on Racine, half minute out.

Sound of gunfire.

FRANK (*on radio*): Sully's hit, Lou.

GOLD: Oh, God . . . Where are you . . . ?

FRANK (*on radio*): Sully's hit bad . . .

OLCOTT: Stuck on the second floor.

GOLD: Where is he? Where's Sullivan?

RADIO: Homicide. I'm on the corner of Fourth. Can you see my lights?

GOLD: Where's Sullivan?

SENNA (*to walkie*): Stay out. Don't come in. Stay out . . .

GOLD *takes the walkie.*

GOLD (*to walkie*): Tim . . . It's Bobby . . . Can you hear me . . . ? I'm going after Sullivan.

A patrol car speeds up the street toward the scene of the shoot-out. As it rounds the corner, it is hit by a spray of gunfire.

SENNA (*rising as the screeching car is hit*): Oh God . . . Charlie, gimme some cover. You two guys get your ass over here.

The car crashes into another police car and bursts into flames. SENNA, OLCOTT, GOLD *run out.* OLCOTT *is shot.*

OLCOTT: I'm hit.

SENNA: Bobby, go for cover, I got him.

GOLD: I'm going. I'm going.

BATES *and* BROWN *come out with wounded officer.*

Ambulance arrives.

BATES: Can we get some help with this kid. Can we get some help over here.

GOLD *runs into the building.*

Interior: Building—Night

GOLD *runs through hallway.*

GOLD *runs up a flight of stairs.*

GOLD *reaches the next floor and moves toward the sounds of voices and gunfire.*

Interior: Stairwell—Night

FRANK *is calling on radio while* JAMES *is bent over* SULLIVAN, *who is lying in a pool of blood.*

FRANK (*to radio*): Yo, where's the backup? Where's the backup?

GOLD *runs into stairwell, cradles Sullivan's head.*

SULLIVAN: I got to get some blood, here.

GOLD: We're working on it. Can we get some help here?

FRANK (*to radio*): Lou . . . Lou, where is the ambulance?

SULLIVAN: He shot the gun dry. I said, "Don't be doing that."
Because you move around, and there's his partner. Do you see,
Bobby?

GOLD: Hold on, Tim.

SULLIVAN: Do you see, Bobby? Although somebody told him
to do that, but who would do that, Bob?

GOLD: Where are the medics?

SULLIVAN: Oh God.

GOLD: Hold on, Tim.

SULLIVAN: Do you know what I'm talking about?

GOLD: Yeah. Yeah. That's right.

JAMES: Frankie, what does the Lou say?

SULLIVAN: Do you know what I'm talking about?

GOLD: Yes I do.

SULLIVAN: 'Cause it, finally, it doesn't make a difference. If
you do or you don't. I swear to Christ I don't know what they're

talking about. If you're moved, there's someone doing it. Doesn't that have to be right?

GOLD: Yes it does.

FRANK (*to radio*): Can we get some help up here, Lou.

SULLIVAN: Bob . . . Bob . . . Bobby . . . You remember that girl that time . . . ? Bob.

GOLD: Tim . . . ?

GOLD *kisses Sullivan's head. He reaches for his gun and flashlight and heads out toward the gunfire.*

GOLD: You shot my partner, you fucking nigger . . . I'm going to kill you.

Two paramedics run in as GOLD *runs out.*

JAMES: Get low! . . . Get low . . .

Interior: Building—Night

GOLD *runs into the room. He sees a door closing, fires at it, and runs in pursuit.*

Interior: Building—Night

GOLD *comes through the door and sees* RANDOLPH *running away below him with the ladder falling down from the loft level where he stands.*

GOLD *holsters his gun and flashlight and jumps onto rope in the pulley.*

The rope stops short on the pulley block, causing GOLD *to fall to the floor and lose his gun.* GOLD *runs after* RANDOLPH, *not realizing his gun is gone. He descends the stairs to a lower level.*

GOLD *enters a maze of tunnels in the basement. He hears a sound and reaches for his gun, but it is gone. He turns off his flashlight, looks around, sees a length of chain, and takes it for a weapon.*

GOLD *walks softly through a tunnel, heads in the direction of the sound.*

GOLD *emerges from a tunnel and sees* RANDOLPH *running in the distance. He goes to head* RANDOLPH *off.*

GOLD *comes out of another tunnel, turns his flashlight on, sees a swaying piece of hanging chain, and moves on.*

Wending his way through the labyrinth, GOLD *is attracted by the sounds of metal being wrenched.*

Around a corner, over Gold's shoulder, RANDOLPH *is levering off a metal grate. Light coming from above indicates that the grate leads up to the street level and to freedom.* RANDOLPH, *exhausted, stops for a moment to catch his breath.*

GOLD, *holding the chain, walks onto a floor full of coal.*

The coal crunches under his feet.

Gold's point of view: RANDOLPH, *holding the lever, turns toward the sound.*

He levels his gun on GOLD.

Randolph's point of view: GOLD *standing, holding the chain.*

RANDOLPH *fires at* GOLD. GOLD *falls.*

RANDOLPH: You came for me, motherfucker. What did you want me for?

GOLD: I came to kill you.

RANDOLPH: Well, you forgot your gun, Jim, where's your gun . . . ?

Voice-over: a siren outside the building.

RANDOLPH: That's Death calling, baby. For you and for me. Sh'I use you, bargain my way out of here?

GOLD: You know they won't bargain for me.

RANDOLPH *goes back to working on the grate.*

RANDOLPH: Z'at so? Well, then, I guess I best had help myself . . .

GOLD: You sorry fucken sack of shit. You shot my partner.

RANDOLPH: Yeah, man, you could of paid me *back*, you'd brought your gun . . . See, that's your *mistake*, maan . . . what's your name . . . ?

GOLD: Gold. Robert Gold.

RANDOLPH *takes a momentary breather.*

RANDOLPH: Well, on my way, Mr. Gold, you see, I'm just 'bout *out* of here . . . I got a *moment*, you wanna tell me your last thought . . . ?

GOLD: No.

RANDOLPH: You want to beg for your life?

GOLD: No.

RANDOLPH: "No"?

GOLD: It's not worth anything.

RANDOLPH: Ain't that a shame, then. After all your trials. It come to nothing.

> RANDOLPH *goes back to working on the grate. He stops to catch his breath.*

Yeah, these motherfuckers got lucky. N'hour ago, I'd of been on a plane and long gone outta here.

GOLD: No, you weren't going nowhere.

> RANDOLPH *goes back to working on the grate. He stops to catch his breath.*

RANDOLPH: The fuck you, you know, man? My momma had it all set up, the ticket, the passport. I woulda been long gone outta here. But that's alright. Now I gotta do it the hard way. You know?

GOLD: Yeah, I know it all.

RANDOLPH: Oh, you know, huh? One Smart Kike. Ain'tcha, Mr. Gold? All you forgot. If you want to *kill* me, you best come armed.

RANDOLPH *gets the grate off the hinges.*

He prepares to start out of the grate.

GOLD: Randolph. Randolph. Your mother turned you in.

Beat.

RANDOLPH (*laughs*): Later, baby—

GOLD: You know she did it. How else did we find you here?

Beat.

RANDOLPH, *starting out the grate, turns back to* GOLD.

RANDOLPH: You're a lying motherfucker. You don't *know* my mother. You ain't never *seen* my mother.

He shoots GOLD.

RANDOLPH: *Look* at you, maan, you a piece of shit.

GOLD *takes the handkerchief, starts to sop up the blood from his wound. Loudspeaker comes on, "You have three minutes to surrender or we are going to take the building. Randolph. Do you hear me? You have three minutes."*

GOLD: That's right. I'm a piece of shit. It's all a piece of shit. I killed my partner. And your momma turned you in, man.

RANDOLPH: Don't die with a lie on your lips, maan.

GOLD *nods. He takes the fake passport out of his shirt pocket, throws it at* RANDOLPH.

GOLD: You want your passport? I got it. It's a phoney. All that shit, man—we made it up. Look at it. Your momma turned you over, Man. Look at it! That's right.

RANDOLPH *picks it up.*

Insert: The passport marked FORGED DOCUMENT OFFICIAL USE ONLY.

Close-up: RANDOLPH *looking at the passport.*

GOLD, *looking at him.*

Beat.

Extreme close-up: RANDOLPH, *looking at the passport.*

Close-up: GOLD.

RANDOLPH, *looking lost, takes a tentative step toward* GOLD.

Exterior: Building opposite—Night

The back of an F.B.I. jacket, as a SNIPER *moves into posi-*

tion. The sniper's eye moves closer into the eyepiece. Pan down to his trigger finger tightening.

Interior: Loft warehouse, continued—Night

RANDOLPH *stepping forward.*

The window, bathed in light, shattering with the bullet.

Extreme close-up: Randolph's face, surprised, dropping out of frame.

Close-up: GOLD *looking up at the falling* RANDOLPH.

Randolph's body falling to the floor.

GOLD *and* RANDOLPH, *who is dying.*

RANDOLPH: God . . . God . . . Help me . . . What did you do to me?

Sound of the door being blown down by explosives. The room is bathed in light, the sound of men shouting orders. GOLD *looks around.*

Close-up: S.W.A.T. team member.

GOLD *and* RANDOLPH. GOLD *looks around.*

The windows blown in, men coming in through the windows, S.W.A.T. teams rushing in through the doors.

GOLD *holding Randolph's head.*

Two S.W.A.T. men advance on GOLD.

GOLD: Don't hurt him . . . don't hurt him . . .

The men roughly separate RANDOLPH, *pointing guns at him.*

Wide angle of the scene in the room, medical personnel entering. Spotlights, police officers crowd in to look on. Eventually they obscure the scene and it goes to black.

Interior: Squad room—Day

Two policemen are talking; they sense something and look away from the camera. Rack focus to GOLD, *who is coming into the police station.*

Camera tracks back as GOLD, *walking with a cane, comes into the station.* OLCOTT *and* JAMES *are going out of the station, followed by* CURRAN. *They stop their conversation and look at* GOLD.

OLCOTT: Hey, Bob.

Beat.

GOLD: Hello.

Pause.

OLCOTT: I'm sorry about Sullivan.

GOLD: Yeah.

JAMES: We got to roll.

OLCOTT: Yeah. Maybe I'll see you later. Have some coffee . . .

CURRAN: See ya around, Bob.

They walk on.

GOLD: Yeah.

GOLD *walks into the hall.*

Interior: Police station hall—Day

Action continues from preceding scene. As GOLD *enters the hall,* SENNA *is coming out of the homicide squad room.*

SENNA: We solved your case for you.

FRANK *comes out of the squadroom, followed by* BATES *and the* JUVENILE OFFICER *and the two* YOUNG BOYS.

YOUNG BOY: I told you why they killed her, man, she had that *fortune* in her basement . . .

The BOYS *walk on.* SENNA *turns back to* GOLD.

SENNA: You're off *homicide.* (*Beat.*) You're off . . .

The BOYS *turn back to address* GOLD.

YOUNG BOY: I would of *got* it, too, that *dog* hadn't scairt me off . . .

The YOUNG BOYS *walk on, leaving* GOLD *alone. Hold on him for a moment. He sees something out of the corner of his eye.*

Angle: point of view—the GROUNDER, *in prison uniform and chains, being led down the hall by two state troopers. The* GROUNDER *looks at him and nods.*

Angle: GOLD *looks at the* GROUNDER.

OFFICER *walks up to* GOLD *and hands him folder of evidence.*

OFFICER (*offscreen*): We've been holding this for you.

GOLD *opens the folder.*

*Insert: A flyer with a picture of a pigeon—*GROFAZT PIGEON FEEDS—NUTRITION, QUALITY, VALUE.

GOLD *looks up to see the* GROUNDER *as he is led away.*

Hold on GOLD.